What people are

Kabbalah and Healing

The Perennial Tradition teaches that all that is true, is true always and everywhere. Kabbalah is part of this eternal wisdom, a way of describing and understanding the patterns of the universe for the purposes of healing our relationships with God, ourselves, each other and the Earth.

This is an oral tradition, intended to be updated by each generation's teachers. As a woman and a Universal Christian rather than a Jewish man, Maggy is a much-needed 21st century pioneer of this important work.
Fr Richard Rohr

Kabbalah is often misunderstood as either a closed, orthodox tradition or a cliquey New Age fad. But for the discerning student Kabbalah, like the Enneagram, is a neutral language of transformation available for anyone with a curious mind and an open heart. When a hospital chaplain told Maggy Whitehouse that her dying husband, an atheist, would not go to heaven, her middling distance from traditional Christianity widened into a chasm. She turned to Judaic Mysticism as a bridge. In Kabbalah she found not only a return to faith, but a doorway into a much deeper, embodied faith — but only after she transformed the blame and resentment she'd projected on to God into renunciation and reconciliation. And for Maggy, Kabbalah was a core part of that healing process. In this down-to-earth and practical book Maggy shows how Kabbalah reveals the patterns of creation that make everything One in the consciousness of the Divine and how, if we won't heal our relationship with whatever we perceive God to be, our own inner demons will prevent any self-development work from being truly transformative or lasting. Kabbalah is

a living tradition, brought into renewed relevance by every generation's teachers. And Maggy is one of the best.
Prof Peter Bolland, author of *The Seven Stone Path: An Everyday Journey to Wisdom* (Balboa Press)

Maggy has lived and breathed this teaching for three whole decades and it shows clearly in both her life and her work. She is witty, down-to-earth and unpretentious.
Jane Struthers, author of *Moonpower* (Eddison Books)

Maggy Whitehouse is one of those authors whose written words actually do speak to you as you read. Some writers have this knack and it makes the reading so much more of an experience, as if you are listening to an audio book. As you read/listen, so you begin to feel the *magic*, and I use that word deliberately.

Unlike many other spiritual/magical books, this is not airy fairy or pie in the sky. It is not just theoretical, but is actually highly practical. Maggy's words are deliberately earthy, gritty, realistic and human. And therefore utterly convincing.

She does not teach that one has to "aspire" or "climb ladders of perfection" to attain what is clearly out of normal human reach. No, she explains, with humour and humanity, how we actually touch the magic "down here", in and through our cracked ego-protecting shells.

This book will draw you into the powerful story of the author's, at times very painful, journey and will immerse you so deeply in it that you will begin to see what she sees and feel what she feels. Why? Because she describes what's happened to you too.

But it's not just about the broken heaps we often end up in/ as. No, it contains something more—a magic—a miraculous truth—a synchronistic dimension that does not come across as nonsense.

And, most importantly, this book is truly inclusive. While

teaching Judaeo-Christian Kabbalah, Maggy in no way seeks to "convert" or "win" you for a particular denomination or faith. She's not hoping to speak to "insiders" or "believers" or "members" of an exclusive club.

I guarantee that if you're genuinely open to her message, whatever background, path or tradition you happen to have arrived here from, you will come away touched and changed.

Mark Townsend, author of *The Pagan Jesus*

Mystically, miraculously, unputdownable. This book is packed full of wisdom, surprise twists, and real experiences of the divine, with a turn of phrase you MUST surely smile at. You can't help but feel you have somehow been drawn along on Maggy's journey into an "effing" essential temple of transformation. Pack a lunch, change starts here.

Deb Rowley, founder of Debx.co.nz

Kabbalah and Healing

A Mystical Guide to Transforming the
Four Pivotal Relationships for Health
and Happiness

Kabbalah and Healing

A Mystical Guide to Transforming the
Four Pivotal Relationships for Health
and Happiness

Maggy Whitehouse

BOOKS

Winchester, UK
Washington, USA

JOHN HUNT PUBLISHING

First published by O-Books, 2020
O-Books is an imprint of John Hunt Publishing Ltd., 3 East St., Alresford,
Hampshire SO24 9EE, UK
office@jhpbooks.com
www.johnhuntpublishing.com
www.o-books.com

For distributor details and how to order please visit the 'Ordering' section on our website.

Text copyright: Maggy Whitehouse 2019

ISBN: 978 1 78904 069 2
978 1 78904 070 8 (ebook)
Library of Congress Control Number: 2019941487

A CIP catalogue record for this book is available from the British Library.

Design: Stuart Davies

UK: Printed and bound by CPI Group (UK) Ltd, Croydon, CR0 4YY
Printed in North America by CPI GPS partners

We operate a distinctive and ethical publishing philosophy in
all areas of our business, from our global network of authors to
production and worldwide distribution.

Contents

Previous Books by Maggy Whitehouse

A Woman's Worth: The Divine Feminine in the Hebrew Bible (978-1780998343)

Prosperity Teachings of the Bible Made Easy (978-1780991078)

From Credit Crunch to Pure Prosperity (978-1846943287)

The Marriage of Jesus (978-1846940088)

Kabbalah Made Easy (978-1846945441)

The Complete Illustrated History of Kabbalah (978-0754817659)

Total Kabbalah (978-0811861373)

The Secret History of Opus Dei (978-1844768875)

Living Kabbalah (978-0600609704)

China By Rail (978-0865650909)

For the Love of Dog (978-1905806485)

The Miracle Man (978-1846944161)

Leaves of the Tree (978-1905806102)

Into the Kingdom (978-1905806171)

The Book of Deborah (978-1905806003)

The Little Book of Prosperity (B0051VUKNU)

The Spiritual Laws of Prosperity (B0055DPJVC)

We must try to understand
the meaning of the age
in which we are called to bear witness.
We must accept the fact
this is an age in which
the cloth is being unwoven.
It is therefore no good trying
to patch. We must, rather,
set up the loom on which
coming generations may
weave new cloth according to
the pattern God provides.
Mother Mary Clare, the Sisters of the Love of God (Anglican
    community founded in Oxford 1967)

Acknowledgments

Heartfelt thanks to: Richard Rohr, Lion Dickinson, Adam Simmonds, David Goddard, John Wadlow, Thomas Keating, Adyashanti, Warren Kenton and all the London Kabbalah group, Suzi Crockford, Cathy Rowlandson, Stephen Pope, Megan Wagner, Queti Knight and Karen Leadbeater for fun, guidance and inspiration.

The healing techniques suggested in this book should only be attempted at the reader's own risk. They carry no medical endorsement and are simply practices that the author herself found to be useful in her healing journey.

Introduction

When my first husband, Henry, was given a diagnosis of metastatic melanoma, back in 1989, and we were both reeling with the shock, I went to the Bible that we had been given on our wedding day and opened it at random, asking for a sign from God.

My finger fell on a line from Psalm 118, *"I shall not die; instead I shall live to praise the Lord my God."*

Of course I interpreted it that Henry wouldn't die, but it meant me. I would not die from this time of trauma, rather I would be shaken out of my lifetime of being an armchair Christian and start to discover what I truly believed. It didn't mean that there wouldn't be a barrowload of crud to get through first.

That wake-up call included a hospital chaplain (I now know he was an angel) telling me that Henry could not go to heaven because he was not a Christian. My reaction was anger, grief and denial but it was the start of a slow transformation. I began to consider this God more deeply and I started to study Judaic mysticism to discover the tradition that Jesus came from. It took my breath away because at its heart, it was Universal and all-embracing.

Move the story on by a decade and my second husband and I had just broken up and I was very sore.

I went up to Birmingham to stay with my mum and we went to Evensong at the church where Henry's ashes had been buried. I remember standing by his grave before the service and thinking, "Where did the hope go? This is the second time my world has been destroyed." Then I went into the church, opened my hymn book and a sheaf of paper fell out. It was the 118th psalm with a sentence underlined. Which line? *"I shall not die, instead I shall live to praise the Lord my God."*

Another decade passed and I was diagnosed with Follicular

Non-Hodgkin Lymphoma, a medically-incurable blood cancer. I went on retreat to the Poor Clares Monastery in North Devon for much-needed time for myself to meditate and pray and I was able to join with the nuns in daily worship. At 5.30 each morning I went to Choir for the morning Angelus followed by Lauds. It's a magical time. "I will awaken the dawn with praise," sings Psalm 108 and this feels like the most ancient of ceremonies, perhaps even similar to the Egyptian Pharaohs calling the sun to rise again.

On the last morning, for some reason, I left the nuns' chapel before the end. I paused at the back of the main church to look at some leaflets and heard them begin to sing again and I realized that I had missed the final part of that morning's prayer.

It was only about five minutes' worth, I was hungry for breakfast and there was really no point in returning but, even so, I knew I must. I retraced my steps and went quietly back into the chapel. There, I fumbled a bit, trying to find the place in the prayer book and Sister Maximilian came over to help me.

One of the sisters is Swedish and I had noticed that she sometimes sang verses of the liturgy out of order. Just as I got to the right page in the book, it was her turn to sing. She sang one particular line and the rest of the nuns stopped dead because it was the "wrong" line.

They started again at the beginning of that psalm.

Which one?

Psalm 118.

Which line did the sister sing out of turn?

"I shall not die, instead I shall live to praise the Lord my God."

I finally realized that it was time to start listening to what God had been trying to yell in my ear all along. It took three wake-up calls to do it, but I was finally listening.

It's fair to say that there were many days after that which had an anoraked, hatted, gloved and fearsome Maggy stomping her way across Dartmoor in wind and rain yelling, "I shall not effing die! I shall effing live to effing praise the Lord my God!" but every time I did that, I would start laughing and that's the best part about it. Because I had finally healed what this book calls the first relationship. God laughed with me. Not at me or about me but with me, and we walked hand-in-hand on the whole journey from there.

This book comes from a combination of what I learnt during those years with cancer and my studies of the Judaeo-Christian mystical tradition of Kabbalah. In chapter sixteen I have included some more of my own healing journey.

But first things first—I'm not Jewish and I'm a woman. For many folk both of these are no-nos from the start when it comes to Kabbalah. An orthodox Jew will tell you that Kabbalah may only be studied by a man over the age of 40.

In addition to that, I may be thought to be simplifying a complex ancient tradition which requires you to be able to read and understand Hebrew texts before you even start.

My response is that neither of these views are supported by the true nature of Kabbalah.

Kabbalah is the Hebrew word for "receive". It is an oral tradition which updates for all times. This is the whole point—that it is a system intended to work for all peoples in all ages. The tradition is held true to itself by adherence to its scaffolding, the diagrams known as the Tree of Life and Jacob's Ladder. These are what prevent this perennial wisdom teaching from becoming mere Chinese Whispers.

For many years Kabbalah was studied in secret (it is the root of the word Cabal which is associated with intrigue and secrecy). But in the 21st century, the cat is well and truly out of the bag for better or for worse, with all kinds of groups and societies—both good and maybe not-so-good—studying and teaching worldwide.

Of course, most of the groups are claiming that all the others are wrong, which is how the human ego works. They are not all wrong; they are just different styles on the same clothes horse. If you like stripes you'll go for one, if you like spots, you'll go for another.

There are hundreds of books and groups about studying Kabbalah and, if you are interested, you will find the one that suits you with the nuances, the Biblical adherence—or not—and the beliefs of its author. But you should also find that the Tree of Life is always present. If it isn't, then the house is built without scaffolding.

Scaffolding is like a skeleton. It's pretty similar for all mammals, just that some of us have tails that show and some don't, some of us walk upright and some don't. As humans, we can be black, white, brown, orange, gay, straight, transgender—whatever—on that scaffolding and we will all be children of the same God because, ultimately, Kabbalah is about finding our soul and spirit—neither of which gives a rap about our gender, our sexuality, our race or colour or creed.

Only the ego does that.

What I have discovered, over more than a quarter of a century of study, teaching and writing books on Kabbalah is that, used as a tool for inspiration, it is a magical loom on which we can weave our healing—and from that healing, we become an agent of healing for the World. Kabbalah tells us exactly where, when, how and why we may be out of alignment with health, finances and relationships and, just as importantly, how to realign ourselves.

So this is a book of information matched with some experience about what I've learnt over nearly half a lifetime. It began with chronic lack of self-esteem which, in turn, led to many a humiliation, widowhood, shark attack, failed emigration, debt, divorce, shame, misery, hatred and what the doctors called an incurable illness which now no longer exists. It can be summed up, in a way, by how the first eight aspects led to the final one and how Kabbalah taught me how to heal them, from finish to start. After all, "incurable" surely means "curable from within".

My prayer is that you will be able to use the teaching in this book to bypass most, if not all, of the above sources of suffering and find your own true healing.

I have included many of the techniques which I have found invaluable in my own continuing healing. These are simply proffered as suggestions; they are not medically proven to work nor guaranteed. You may well find other techniques which work better for you. However, information alone is not much use, it is experience which transforms information into knowledge and makes it real. Hopefully, you will try some, if not all, of the suggested techniques in this book to create your own inner knowing.

On this journey, we won't be using much Hebrew, we won't be following the 613 laws of the Hebrew Testament, we won't be reciting any multi-lettered names of God. All of those are fine and dandy if they are part of your culture and your healing but they have not been a part of mine and, ultimately, the only story you can tell with any validity is your own.

What we will be doing is using this ancient scaffolding in a way that is totally appropriate for the 21st century, whatever your belief system, culture or status. Properly used, it will work for all of us because that's what it's designed to do.

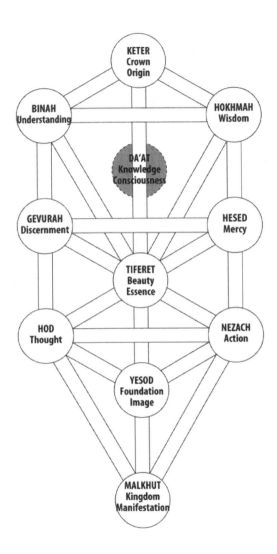

Part One

The Four Relationships

Chapter One

The Mystical Tradition

All of creation is One.

All of life is relationship.

At first sight those two statements appear to contradict each other; if we are all One then we cannot be in relationship, for being in a relationship requires there to be an Other.

And yet, each cell in our bodies is both complete and in relationship with the others. When that relationship falls apart, and is not healed, the whole is in danger of becoming diseased.

The body strives to heal, to unify and re-weave. A cut on the finger of someone dying of cancer will still mend unless it, itself, is poisoned.

We have thousands of relationships within our bodies, within our souls, within our minds, within our brains. All of them make up the form that is "us" and they dictate the health of the whole.

All pure relationships enhance the whole, whether that is the body, the soul or the Universe. All adulterated relationships create tears in the fabric of creation.

Each human, each animal, each plant, each breath of wind has its place in our Universe. Whatever we are and do may have the tiniest of effects but a drop of love or a drop of poison expands either from our physical finger to our heart or via our words to our children and friends and to their friends and onwards.

Yes, a drop of antiseptic can kill the poison. But who is to apply that antiseptic but you?

What makes us unique on this planet is that we are the only beings that can choose whether we spread love or poison. Mostly, we have chosen to create holes, from holes in the ozone layer to holes in our ability to love or to discern and, because those holes are familiar, they become part of our whole. Nearly all those choices are made unconsciously or subconsciously but they are still choices even if the choice was not to choose.

We are designed, as animals, to seek the familiar because it feels safe. We are comfortable hanging out with people who share our opinions so that if our view or action is attacked by an other, then we have safety in numbers and our side will fight for and with us. This is the law of fight or flight—us and them. It is natural to all animals as a survival mechanism.

The human soul transcends the need to be part of this tribal system and the tribe doesn't like that which is why spiritual growth is neither convenient nor comfortable.

Ironically, quite often when we humans believe that we are speaking or working from our soul (as in religion), we are actually speaking or working from our ego. To understand that is to understand why we humans got into such a mess about the idea of God. The idea of "my religion" and "your religion" are not and never can be the view of the soul.

You can tell when the two have become mixed for a person will tell you that they are working from the heart or are "soul based". Neither the heart nor the soul have any need to inform you of that; the ego does. And the ego is lying.

Kabbalah and the Four Relationships

Kabbalah is not a religion; it is a loom for weaving a unified cloth of many colours showing us what aspects of ourselves are strong and what aspects are unravelling. It helps us to rediscover what religion is meant to be, stripping off the outmoded forms of older times and showing a clear strong scaffolding to create the appropriate tapestry of blessings for our lives today.

The loom originated as the Menorah, a seven-branched candlestick in the Holy of Holies in the first temple of the Hebrews. Nowadays it is known as the Tree of Life and the four relationships that we need to transform for healing relate to the four *sefirot* (Hebrew for "sphere") on the central column of consciousness of the Tree.

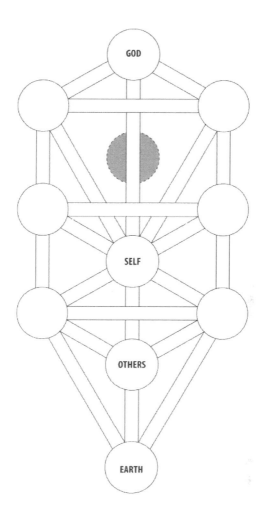

The four relationships are

- With God
- With Ourselves
- With Others
- With the Earth.

The earthly relationship includes all things physical, including our own bodies.

Most people perceive the Tree of Life as being upright, with its roots in the earth just like a physical tree. But the inner mystical teaching is that it is inverted—with its taproot being our link to the Divine, its trunk our spirit, its branches our psyches and its leaves, flowers and fruits the manifestation of our physical lives. The root is the first and all-important source of nourishment, while the leaves, flowers and fruits are fragile and transitory. However, all three other levels can and will be renewed constantly when the root is strong. This is why our first focus in this book will be on healing our relationship with the Divine. From that, all other relationships can and will heal themselves.

If your first thought is, "My relationship with God is fine," and yet you are, in any way, hurt, disappointed, broke, sick or in pain, please think again.

The First Relationship

A healthy relationship with God is purely personal. More than that, a totally healthy relationship with God is union with the Divine, for God and we are extensions of each other. However, this feeling of unity is rare. Fortunately a loving one-to-one relationship is still a powerfully healing one.

The element of this Kabbalistic level on the Tree of Life is Fire and it is from this that we get the phrase "the healing fires of Grace". Fire to humanity represents light and warmth, although fire can also be terrifying because it destroys the known and the familiar and we judge that as being wrong. But a forest fire opens seeds which if not burnt would not grow. Divinity is as transformative as fire and that is why we humans have attempted to control it with religion so that we can deny it any but the power that we want it to have—which renders it useless and often harmful. To paraphrase CS Lewis, writing of Aslan, the Christ figure in the Narnia books, "God is not a tame lion."

If we are fortunate enough to live in a family which has a

direct, loving relationship with the Divine, then we will learn how to experience the same—but this is the exception rather than the rule. God is in the space between us and our thoughts and it is these spaces which are all-important. Without spaces between the notes, there could be no music, only continual noise. A healed relationship with the Divine is like participating in a celestial symphony—a Divine Dance of notes and spaces in perfect harmony. We are born in this space but, unless we are natural mystics or are taught the importance of stillness, it closes as we grow. A young child communicates easily with higher and invisible worlds until he or she is taught that these are fictional or inappropriate. When I was nine, I had a mystical experience in Church which enveloped me in the colours, sounds, touch and taste of Love—and already I knew better than to tell anyone about it because by that age I knew that it would be dismissed and destroyed or even thought heretical, and it was too real and too precious to risk having it shattered.

What is deemed appropriate for us to believe in is taught and internalized very young and lodged in what Freud called our super ego. It becomes truth which is why humanity constantly makes God in its own image instead of the other way around.

It follows that if we don't believe that there is a God at all, then there cannot be one, so anyone of faith has to be deluded. An atheist once said to me, "You seem like a fairly intelligent person; why don't you just use your brain and realize that there's nothing?" If I'd been quick-witted, I'd have answered that God has nothing to do with the brain and everything to do with the soul but it is perhaps as well that I didn't because nobody likes a smart-arse.

Our view of God is vital because who and what we perceive God to be will tell us clearly who we perceive ourselves and others to be. It will also dictate whether or not we think this is a safe world. When the one-to-one or unified relationship with God is sound, we will experience divinity, love God, love ourselves, love others and love the planet. But most orthodox religion teaches us of a patriarchal King God whom we must both fear and love subserviently. From that foundation, we learn to despise ourselves, to despise and fear others who hold different beliefs and to dominate and fear the physical. If there were walls in heaven, God would be banging His/Her head on them at that one.

The Second Relationship

Our relationship with ourselves is a mix of personal and impersonal because we have our own beliefs and we also take on the projections of others as being what we believe to be "us".

"Personal" simply describes when we feel connected but not necessarily protected. "Impersonal" is the other way around; when we will go with the tribe's view or the safest option even if it feels uncomfortable. Our soul knows who we are as expressions of the Divine but our ego learns who others think we are supposed to be through our interactions with our parents, carers, teachers and peers. We take in those opinions and make them ours through repetition, often at great cost to the soul.

This relationship relates to spirit in Kabbalah, the element of Air. We are spiritual beings who have temporarily come to Earth for a limited span of time in a body. Our spirit is part of the great Oneness and feeds our soul, which lives in the levels of water and spirit, fed directly from divinity if we allow it to be.

The second relationship is complicated by its existence on three levels. There is who we think we are (ego-self), who we really are (true self), and who we were born with the potential to become (higher self). The vast majority of people spend their lives being who they think they are, as learnt from their interactions with others.

When I was a child much of my identity came from protecting my mother who was agoraphobic. I learnt to tell lies to cover up for her fear because she wanted to keep it hidden. This codependent behaviour brought only transient happiness to either of us as it couldn't lead to any true healing and it was disastrous for my self-esteem. It was only after I broke away, physically, moving to another country, where I had to think anew without family ties and habits, that the illusion could crash and both my mother and I were forced to face the truth about ourselves. Both of us experienced extremely difficult times but both of us came through stronger, happier and healthier as a result. We found out who we really were and began to love and even like ourselves.

The Third Relationship

Once we have healed our relationship with God and with ourselves, there is much less to do in order to heal our relationship with others because we begin to understand that there is no other; there is only an extension of God-in-us. If we have done neither, this third world of the psyche, symbolized by Water, will most likely be haphazard and troubled instead of calm.

The relationship with others is a complete blend of personal and impersonal and is driven both from above and below. If we feel confident in ourselves and our Source, we will work in harmony with others, seeing them as equals and as brother or sister. If we are not and it is a question of survival of the fittest, we will destroy others for our own needs; similarly, if others' perceptions of who we believe ourselves to be form a threat to our lifestyle, their views will be feared, dismissed, despised or hated.

This relationship will work in accord with those whom we believe share our views both about us and about the world so that we can feel more connected and protected. However, we will also project our beliefs about God, them and us on to everyone we meet in order to draw to us those people who will prove those beliefs to be true. This will frequently make us feel disconnected but the ego, which is a meld of the two lower worlds, is wired to be far more interested in being right and being safe than it is about being happy.

In my younger years, I thought I had several relationships with men but later I was able to see that I only had one. I recreated exactly the same relationship with different boyfriends and partners—which was an extension of the pattern that my parents and I had created between us.

The pattern was: attraction; ignore or discount incompatibilities and compromise in order to feel loved; commit; find I would have to subsume myself and my talents in order to maintain harmony; be unable to deny my own creativity; be found over-powerful, wrong or wanting and be pushed away. I got so accustomed to this pattern that my first husband had to die and my second husband had to leave before I allowed myself to be alerted to it. One of the most potent realizations that I had changed my inner beliefs was when my third husband said he prayed that, when we were very old, I would be the first of us to die so that I would never have to be left again. This marriage is still happy and stable after twice as many years as the other two combined so excuse me for a moment while I do a quick happy dance.

The Fourth Relationship

Our relationship with the Earth is either personal or impersonal and powerfully linked with survival. In past times we worked closely with the land and the cycles of life and death and we understood how fragile and precious physical reality was. Before hospitals, hot running water, medicines—both herbal and chemical—antibiotics and many other incredible inventions and adaptations, just one insect bite or cut could easily lead to death.

In this modern world, some of us still have that connection with the planet and feel threatened by the future with regard to climate change, pollution and the like. This can break out into our relationship with others in that we blame and shame those we see responsible for hurting our Mother Earth and her creatures.

To save our environment we have to work together and it is often hard for those passionate about the planet to understand that hostility, anger and pushing against the others who don't care is energetically as destructive as the waste products being produced. To work together in harmony, there must be peace within. The external problem is only ever a reflection of the internal one.

When I was diagnosed with cancer it was a tremendous wake-up call. It was a form of the disease that I could easily have blamed on insecticides and external pollutions but I knew in my soul that this was a far deeper issue. The level of shame I felt, as "a spiritual person", was a powerful clue about the amount of pride I carried—and pride is always a block to divinity. So I knew that I had to start again to heal another level of my relationship with God, myself and others. It may well have been that pesticides contributed to the disease but I knew that outer poisons could only have connected with inner ones which I had been carrying for a very long time. When I went within, I could locate that poison hiding in plain sight and trace it backwards and inwards to its source. This is what I believe we all have to do before our planet can heal. Luckily one small step in the right direction can move mountains.

Those of us who are disconnected from the planet will continue to take what we want, often without any consideration, feeling secure that there will always be enough or simply not caring about a future generation. That is how the ego works. But Kabbalah teaches that it only takes 1% of humanity to move in the right direction for the tide to turn and this is achievable.

It is also important to understand that should it come down to basic apocalyptic survival, it would be a rare person who did not take what they needed at whatever cost.

Money

We can start our healing in any of the four relationships and it will permeate through to the other levels. But there is another pivotal element that runs through all of our relationships, affecting every aspect, and that is money.

For most of us, nowadays, survival equates to money and economics certainly dictates most of how humanity treats the planet and most of our conscious and unconscious behaviour towards her.

However, our attitudes towards money reveal much about our relationship with God, with ourselves and with others as well as with the Earth.

- In our relationship with God, money relates to power or control.
- In our relationship with ourselves, money relates to worth.
- In our relationship with others, money relates to fairness.
- In our relationship with the Earth, money relates to survival.

Our allotment of time on Earth is limited and precious, and our choices of how to use our life force here express our meaning and purpose. It is a rare person who does not trade some of their life force for money or use the concepts of economic security as a paradigm of success. Money today is a god and is both worshipped and reviled as such.

Money is a human-created representation of the flow of abundance and hatred of it cuts our own links to abundance— and to the Earth herself. If the idea of linking money with the four relationships is repugnant to you, it simply shows how very powerful a hatred of money and all it is perceived to stand for is in the unconscious mind of society and how vital the healing of our relationship with it is to our world.

The critical thing to remember about money is that less than

2% of it is in physical notes or coins; all of the rest exists in the world of Yezirah as a thought-form. This is the world of emotions and imagination. Therefore money is critically affected by our thoughts and feelings about it. At the very least, a neutral stance on money is required in order to be prosperous and a view that we don't want money ourselves can end up being a surprisingly selfish one; after all, how can we prosper others if we are not prosperous ourselves?

For a full breakdown on healing money issues, please see my book, *From Credit Crunch to Pure Prosperity* (O-Books).

The Four Relationships and Health

Each of the four relationships permeates the others so both health and dis-ease in one will flow through to another. Everything is connected. Your beliefs about yourself affect your relationship with the Universe, with others and with your prosperity and finances. Perfect health depends on the right relationship between all four levels.

- If we worship a specific God, we will despise and wage psychological or physical war on those who don't.
- If we worship ourselves, we will demand admiration to demonstrate that worth.
- If we worship others, we will sacrifice ourselves for their approval.
- If we worship physical things, we will harm the planet by our need to possess more and more of them.

It is even simpler when we dwell in hatred. That is what the legend of eating of the tree of knowledge of good and evil is about: it's not a one-off situation of original sin (which is a third century construction invented by St Augustine and is unknown in the Jewish faith) but an exhortation to watch our ego's opinions in every moment. The moment we take the higher ground over religion, politics or the economy we are judging right and wrong according to our own criteria and we are setting ourselves up as superior over "the other" so that we can, if we want, wallow in righteous anger. It doesn't matter how accurate we may be in our belief; we have just taken another hearty bite out of that forbidden fruit which destroys any chance of resolution of conflict or healthy relationship.

If we hate, resent or despise a specific God, we cut ourselves off from the Whole and therefore life force. It follows that if we hate, resent or despise ourselves, others or the physical world (and/or money), we cut ourselves off from the Whole and therefore life force.

It is time to reconnect and heal, for our healing is the world's healing. Let us set out the criteria of how Kabbalah can help.

Chapter Two

The Patterns of the Universe

Let's begin at the beginning, not as the Bible is written but in practical, down-to-earth terms in order to see how and why we came to believe what we did and we do.

In the first centuries of homo sapiens, there really wasn't very much to do in the evenings. You didn't have a lot of light, you didn't have books or TV or the Internet. All you had was the firelight, your companions and the night sky. In the temperate regions you probably had rain and in the desert regions you probably had thirst, which was worse.

You didn't have a lot to talk about either. Unless you had met a wolf or a lion that day it would have been pretty routine stuff — find or hunt food, make or mend a basket, fetch water, deal with your mother-in-law — hardly useful topics of conversation when everyone you know is sat around that fireside with you and politics hasn't been invented yet. To be fair, a lion might have created discussion for weeks though mostly it would have been about how to get rid of the darn thing because if you didn't, it would eat you. Political correctness is not a big factor when it comes to survival.

Generally, had we been there, most of us would have passed the time before sleeping by watching the sky or the flames in the fire and we would talk about what we knew and what we'd observed and perhaps, even, make up stories about it to entertain ourselves and the others.

As time went past, those stories took on patterns, based on our observations — simple things like which of the stars moved and which didn't. Why did some move? Someone would certainly ask that question and if you wanted to keep your place by the fire, you'd need to find an answer.

And we noticed other patterns of creation, too; the seasons, the phases of the Moon, what certain kinds of clouds meant and how soon that meant rain and how diseases manifested and progressed or were healed. We noted how life seemed to organize itself in threes—three primary colours for a start and less tangible things like beginnings, middles and endings and three dimensions of up, down and sideways to everything visible. We observed four basic elements—fire, air, water and earth—as well as four seasons and four compass points.

We noted that tens must be important because they helped us to count on our fingers and toes and we liked sevens because of things like the seven visible, moving (to us) celestial objects, seven colours of the rainbow, seven notes on the musical scale and the seven directions (left, right, up, down, forward, back and centre).

And we passed this knowledge on to our children and to anyone else who was interested—and probably to quite a few who weren't.

In addition, we noticed patterns in people; how some folk were more aggressive than others; some were leaders, some were craftsmen or women, some were more playful or more sullen. And, those of us who were truly interested in all this stuff—and had time to ponder, given how challenging it was merely to survive in those days—would begin to notice how the patterns interacted with the moving objects in the sky and with each other. Over decades, we might observe that the moving star in the sky which had a red tinge to it seemed to affect some people's passions, and even aggression, and the moving star in the sky which had a blue tinge seemed to have a definite effect on general friskiness.

We might even have thought that it was quite clever and possibly even ponder who or what worked it out in the first place. The logical answer to that would be our ancestors; those folk who had died but who might still have some interest in us.

If we asked them for help when we needed it, they might agree.

There would also be some living folk who seemed to be able to affect the weave of the pattern themselves with prayers, meditations, rituals or just through their emotions. They would become known as shamans or priests and we would ask them to invoke the ancestors for us. They would be able to explain that it was much bigger than that; that there was some Consciousness behind all of this and that it could be contacted and transmitted. And although some of these shamans would have been benign and used their interaction with the Great Pattern for good, some of them might use the power they had to control people. And many of them would have focused on one thread in the pattern— one particular god, if you like—rather than the whole thing. And being human we would have developed our favourite and our least favourite gods and worshipped the one that suited us, rejecting the ones that didn't; and that's when we started the whole "My god is bigger than your god" shebang.

Nobody read or wrote because there really wasn't anything but account tallies that needed to be written or understood in those days; it was all word of mouth and because most of us don't want to sit in silence, learning to receive and understand the wisdom of the Great Pattern (or the various smaller patterns), because we'd got things to do, make and harvest, we preferred to leave it to the priests to invoke It/Them every now and then when we needed help and offer gifts to make It/Them like us. And from then it was a short journey to building places where we could leave those gifts, where the shamans could live and where they could intercede on our behalf and we could get on with our lives.

Next, came those who said they could interpret the mind of the Great Pattern (the moment we believed that It had a mind, we had created It in our own image and that would always bring trouble) and what had been intuition, intended to be received anew day by day, became something to keep doing continually.

After all, if it had worked once, it would work again, surely? There began the Law.

The One Great Pattern

You could say that it was downhill all the way from there but not necessarily so. All through the generations, there have always been those who held to the original pattern, understanding that it was a conscious creative process that recreated the Universe continually, moment by moment. Its whole reality was both One and in relationship with itself. That relationship was the cradle in which creation lay and it was not to be contained, manipulated or even understood. It just is.

The Hebrews were the first people that we know of who built a whole religion on the One Great Pattern rather than its various parts but, even in their writings, they reveal different aspects of the One (the sefirot on the Tree of Life). The Hebrew Testament uses more than a dozen different names or combinations of names to describe God but there are three root ones: *Eheyeh Asher Eheyeh, Elohim* and *Yahweh* from which all the others flow.

The Bible, strange as it may seem, holds the truth of the Great Pattern. It just doesn't tell you that it does. That's because when the texts that form it were written down they were never meant to be taken literally for the next three thousand years. They were meant to be indicators of the patterns on which we could weave the ever-updating present.

In the Book of Exodus, Moses directed the building of the Tabernacle that humanity built/God gave (according to your take on it). This was a structure that showed the simple, consistent basics of the Great Pattern—a kind of skeleton for how life works. Probably, the original intention was so that all shamans or priests could learn generations of knowledge swiftly instead of starting from the beginning all over again. Each generation could start from the same point and, because it was a skeleton on to which you could hang different kinds of skin, hair, clothes, whatever, and observe not only that everyone was different but that also they were, underneath, fundamentally the same. But of course it became set in stone and 99% of people, including the priests, lost the knack of interpreting the weave.

The Hebrews also made a directly visible form of the scaffolding which was known as the *Menorah*. It was a seven-branched candelabrum which showed the simple, mathematical formulae that underpinned the patterns of creation.

Within the design of the Menorah was the template of the Tree of Life and Jacob's Ladder, including four levels for the four basic elements of fire, air, water and earth and a mystical fifth element of consciousness. There were ten aspects which matched our fingers and toes and they were defined in the Ten Commandments—another aspect of our understanding of God which often causes problems.

The Book of Exodus tells us that the commandments were given to Moses three times on Mount Sinai. Most folk think they were given twice but the text is quite clear that it is three. The first time was verbally, the second was written (the mystics tell us) on sapphire and only the third was set in stone. Kabbalistic teaching tells us that the first version of the commandments was oral—in the form of advice on how to weave our lives happily and healthily within the law of Karma—and the second was a more tangible confirmation of the first in order to add a structure to this tradition. It is no coincidence that sapphire and sefira (the singular of "sefirot") have same root letters in Hebrew.

Moses smashed the sapphire commandments on discovering that the Israelites had created an idol to worship while he was away speaking with the Holy One. So, by the time we got to the third set of laws, they were written in stone as commands to be obeyed because humanity had shown that it was not ready to listen to advice—or to do the work required to weave our lives consciously.

This means:

- If we are in direct contact with the Divine we will receive advice and wisdom directly. This communication will be continual and will update according to our situation.
- If we find it hard to understand or trust that communication, then we will be given guidelines for living in a beautiful, transparent structure which can also be updated accordingly.
- If we won't listen then, for our own safety, we must be given laws to obey.

From the last set of commandments came the root of organized religion as we understand it today; where the laws are frequently seen to be far more important than the original impulse of love. Luckily, the original, mystical, loving teachings are still there, woven into the text for us to find if we know how and where to look. The oral tradition is always hidden; you have to want it and be prepared to seek it diligently in order to find it. The human ego wants everything given without effort but that which is revealed too easily will frequently be discounted or abused.

Kabbalah entwines the two first sets of commandments in its structure and we will be looking at those more deeply in a few chapters' time.

Kabbalah is not a religion. However, it is also important to acknowledge how very Jewish it is. For a start, its name comes from the Hebrew letters QBL—so yes, technically it should be called Qabbalah—but the K is more accepted in the 21st century. Jewish folk often believe that Kabbalah belongs to Judaism and we certainly owe the Jewish Nation a huge debt of gratitude for developing it and keeping it pure. But, like Christianity—and the heart of all great faiths—it is a set of principles not tied to any specific religion. The Tree of Life and Jacob's Ladder are both diagrams for living. The tradition is for everyone; it simply works. All you have to do is use the diagram as a loom.

Worshipping the loom is much easier than weaving on it and that's where most religions fall down.

The Underlying Scaffolding or Loom

So let's dive in and see how best to explain this scaffolding. Firstly, the Menorah was updated into two newfangled diagrams in the 13th century by the school of a mystic known as Isaac the Blind in Gerona, Spain. His full name was Rabbi Yitzhak Saggi Nehor (c. 1160–1235). He was given the Aramaic epithet "*Saggi Nehor*" meaning "of Much Light" in the sense of his having excellent eyesight even though he came to be known as Isaac the Blind. I think it's an Aramaic in-joke so we should probably just laugh politely and move on.

It is believed that Rabbi Yitzhak's school of Kabbalah developed as a response to the rationalist philosophy of the school of Maimonides (1135–1204) in Cordoba. Maimonides was a great scholar and teacher who linked the Jewish tradition to Aristotelian doctrine—a very intellectual and somewhat macho teaching—whereas Isaac the Blind and his school veered more towards the line taken by the Greek philosopher Plato and the Neoplatonism which followed him and then added mysticism to the meld.

Just so that we are clear, I'm using the Tree of Life—and its companion, Jacob's Ladder—from the tradition in which I'm trained. It's known as the Toledano Tradition and it takes its roots from a 16th century rabbi called Moses Cordovero.

It probably isn't any better than any other system so, if you already understand Kabbalah from another school, please feel free to reinterpret. However, I, personally, do think it's the best for one simple reason: it is the only tradition that honours the idea that the Universe is perfect.

In the Book of Genesis, when the Elohim wove the Universe, (s)he thought that the end result was "very good". In fact, the Hebrew could justifiably be translated as "exceedingly excellent". And yet, most systems of Kabbalah rely on the idea that God made a bit of a mess of it.

Let me explain. Most Kabbalah that you will come across, including groups like the Kabbalah Centre and Bnai Bruch, are what's known as Lurianic Kabbalah, named after a charismatic rabbi called Isaac Luria who lived in the 16th century. He was Moses Cordovero's student.

When Rabbi Luria was alive, the Jewish nation was still reeling from the Spanish Inquisition, forced conversion, execution by fire and finally expulsion from the Iberian Peninsula. They'd already been kicked out of Britain and many other countries and that would be hard enough for any people, let alone those who truly believed they were God's Chosen Nation.

So the big question of the day was, "Why do bad things happen to good people?"

Luria sought inspiration and the answer that he received is that when God created the Universe, s/he made a mistake. The sefirot or vessels that contained the flow of creation were not strong enough and shattered, creating shards (in Hebrew, *klippot*) which became evil forces that attacked the Universe. These klippot would later become known as demons in Christianity.

If you question a Lurianic Kabbalist nowadays about the "exceedingly excellent" part of Genesis and how this lines up, they will most likely tell you that the shattering of the vessels was also part of God's plan and A Good Thing. Personally, I struggle a little with their logic on that but if the system works for you, then I'm not going to knock it. The loom will work with either system. Another idea that is mooted is that the sefirot shattered because they were unable to pass the light on and that the lesson for humanity is that we have to focus on giving rather than receiving to heal the wounds of the World. That rings a lot of bells and, let's face it, there are a lot of people, groups and societies that could surely benefit from that teaching. However, as I see it, we attempting-to-be-spiritual types in the modern world have somewhat of a culture of giving in order to achieve self-esteem—so that we can feel better about ourselves—and I have had several decades of working with those who had huge prosperity problems because they over-gave without being able to receive for themselves. One of the things in this book is a focus on the importance of balance. We need to receive, appreciate and then give for the whole system to work healthily.

So, I'm going to focus on the earlier form of Kabbalah which is based on the work of Rabbi Luria's teacher, Rabbi Moses Cordovero, also because it is the nearest we can get to the system used when the Bible was written. And as the whole "God Issue" is a huge hole in modern spirituality, and I use a lot of Biblical teachings with Kabbalistic interpretations to try and mend that, this is the most sensible one for me.

Cordovero's tradition was also the one closest to that used in *La Convivencia*, a Spanish phrase that is hard to translate but refers to the "coming together of souls" in Moorish Spain in the 11th and 12th centuries, before Ferdinand and Isabella Christianised the Iberian Peninsula and introduced the Inquisition. The Moors allowed all faiths (though to be fair, they did tax them) and in Moorish Toledo, Cordoba, Genoa and all around Spain and Southern France, mystics of all three Abrahamic faiths met and studied together. More than that, they practised what is known as *Merkabah* meditations together. These are internal ascents to the presence of the Divine, as described in the Books of Exodus, Ezekiel and in the Transfiguration of Jesus in the Gospels. For the mystic, the Book of Revelation is also an internal Merkabah journey.

The nearest we can get to Cordovero's teachings is now known as Toledano Tradition Kabbalah and it was once referred to by a Kabbalistic colleague as "the reunion of the sons of Abraham." Nowadays, I'm glad to say, it is more a reunion of the grandchildren of Abraham of all genders.

This tradition was updated in the 1970s onwards by Kabbalist

Z'ev ben Shimon Halevi who ran a mesoteric group in London, England and spread an updated and comprehensible version of the teaching throughout the world. Halevi has had his fair share of criticism both for opening up the teaching to non-Jewish folk and for restoring Jacob's Ladder to the world. It's believed that this ladder had been present in Kabbalistic teaching pre-Luria but disappeared after his time into the realms of deep esoterica. It was re-revealed in the 1970s for a generation which was beginning to understand, anew, the teachings of Karma or the Law of Attraction.

I benefitted greatly from the Halevi teachings (among others) and am very happy to be one of those updating the tradition again for the 21st century.

Chapter Three

Outlining the Scaffolding

The Tree of Life is a structure showing how the light of creation flows. It begins at *Keter*, Hebrew for the Crown, and flows to *Hokhmah*, Wisdom or Revelation, and then on to *Binah*, Understanding... and then on down the diagram in a zigzag motion.

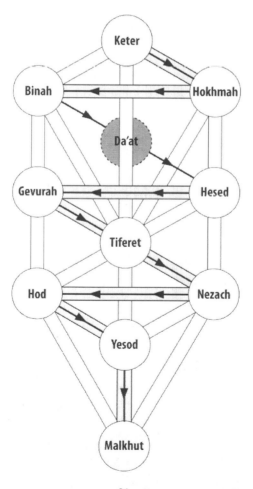

Why is it a zigzag? To demonstrate the duality of existence: Hokhmah and the right-hand side of the Tree are about flow, action, movement, giving, doing and excitement; Binah and the left-hand side of the Tree are about constriction, boundaries, strength, discernment, thought and receiving. We need two sides to ensure that all can be balanced and bring us back to unity. A boiling kettle needs to be switched off or taken off the heat or it will dry up and possibly explode.

The left-hand, restrictive side is associated with the word "no", the feminine and darkness, and the right-hand side is associated with the word "yes", the masculine and light.

Howls of protest frequently emerge from this aspect of the teaching but this is feminine and masculine, not women and men or even female and male. Every single one of us is a mix of masculine and feminine; to be identified as man or woman simply means that we have the physical characteristics of one or the other and even that can be a problem in the modern world which is opening up to transgender consciousness. The Tree of Life is not a judgmental diagram—far from it. If you're a parent or even own a pet, you'll know that when it comes to puppies of any species, the word "no!" is just as important, if not more so, than the word "yes". Without "no" most of us would have died pretty young from all the actions that were not restricted. "No" is simply not as much fun as "yes" and that's a mistake that modern folk often make. Life is not always about fun despite our best efforts to keep ourselves constantly entertained in the Western world. It *is* about joy but that is to be found on the central column and even in the seemingly-darkest of situations.

Without the strength and boundaries of the left-hand side of the Tree, the right-hand one would simply explode in volcanic eruptions everywhere. And without the force and enthusiasm of the right-hand side, the left-hand one would end in paralysis and stasis. They must be in relationship with each other because balance is always the key and that is the purpose of the central column of the Tree.

Even more, each of the sefirot has a balance of both masculine and feminine within it. As the light of creation flowed from Keter, it had to be received in Hokhmah before it could flow on to Binah which, in turn, received it and then flowed it on. This dance of giving, receiving, giving, receiving is the primary pattern of life.

The balance, in all of us, is held on the central column of consciousness. This is where we figuratively "hold things together" and the inspiration behind the phrase "coming to your senses". To come to your senses is to become aware of what is truly happening; picking up messages from your mind, spirit and body. In the modern world we are less accustomed than we used to be to the subtle messages that come from within and without. The central column from *Tiferet* upwards listens to inspiration and the column from Tiferet down listens to instinct or gut feeling. Both are vital levels of consciousness in navigating a healthy and successful life.

Each of the ten sefirot has an attribute and each one represents a level of comprehension. In a nutshell, the top sefira is our contact with the Divine and the bottom sefira is physical reality. In between we have our ego, our thoughts, our actions, our true self, our powers of discrimination, our loving kindness, our knowledge (or lack of it), our understanding and our wisdom, all working in relationship with each other.

When any of these are hopelessly out of balance, dis-ease occurs.

Jacob's Ladder is four Trees of Life interwoven with each other. Each of them has the same ten sefirot and an eleventh one which is, effectively, the window between worlds; the pivotal point of the relationship between them.

To the human the four worlds represent the four relationships:

- *Azilut* (Divinity): The concept of all the aspects of creation and the source of all creation, representing our relationship with the Divine.

- *Beriah* (Spirit): This is the force that begins the actual process, creating the structure of each individual child of the Divine, reflected uniquely in each being, human, animal, plant and even mineral. This uniqueness represents our relationship with ourselves.
- *Yezirah* (Formation): This is the world where skeletal structure is filled out and defined as to whether the creation is to be male, female, furry, mobile, four-legged, two-legged, black, green etc. This also forms the psyche dictating whether this is a being that lives alone or with others, in tribes or strata or herds, and therefore it separates us out and creates "others" for us to be in relationship with.
- *Assiyah* (Physical Manifestation): This is the physical reality of the being on Earth, our relationship with our planet and our means of survival.

The Ladder shows how each of the relationships links and melds with the others, overlapping and therefore spreading healing or dis-ease at each level into the one(s) above or below.

Any reference to "the" Tree of Life is a reference to Yezirah, which is the world representing our psyches and souls. This world is in touch with all three other worlds and it is at this level that we can perceive where the source of any dis-ease may be and give us clues as to how we may be able to clear the imbalance which led to its manifestation.

The Kabbalistic story of creation tells of how the Absolute—God—wanted to experience everything possible in reality rather than simply as a concept. That means everything and includes experiences that we would call "bad" as well as "good". To do so, It had to withdraw Itself in order to create a space—or a womb—of nothingness into which It could breathe the essence of creation. This mystery is the first concept of relationship.

Jacob's Ladder was the result of this breath and the first world, known as Azilut, is the Divine template of a great being known as *Adam Kadmon* — a blueprint of a perfected human being. *Adamah* is the Hebrew for both "earth" and "blood" and is often translated as "red earth". It is a word with no gender ascribed to it although it has long been used as male. The "molecules" which make up Adam Kadmon are the essences of what will become creation including individual, human beings when we descend through the lower worlds to incarnate on the Earth.

Kabbalah teaches that each of us comes from one aspect of Adam Kadmon and each of us has a particular destiny to fulfil whether it is to be the perfect soldier, philosopher, lover, teacher or whatever. This occurs over many lives. Kabbalistic sources disagree on whether our souls have a specific gender but those who say they do not, do still agree that each soul has a tendency towards incarnating as one gender or the other according to its particular destiny. In the modern world, where there is much focus on LGBTQ, it is entirely possible that souls who have incarnated many times as one gender are now beginning an arduous changeover process.

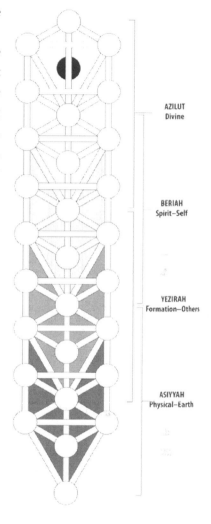

AZILUT
Divine

BERIAH
Spirit–Self

YEZIRAH
Formation–Others

ASIYYAH
Physical–Earth

From Azilut, this world of the Divine Human Being, flowed Beriah the Spiritual World. Beriah is the realm of creation and ideas, so you could say that Azilut was the spark and Beriah the concept. Neither of these two worlds has any form or image, nor operates in time or space, so they are very hard to imagine and even harder to describe. It is said that all that has ever happened and all that will happen are already recorded in Azilut and the upper part of Beriah and all that has ever existed is held safe there, including the presence of everything made extinct from our Earth.

At the Beriatic level, the right-hand side of the Ladder is pure creation and the left-hand is pure destruction—each characteristic being as important as the other and just as dangerous if misused.

As the light flows down and down the Ladder, further into the void/womb and further from its Source, its quality coarsens. Azilut is Fire, Beriah is Air and the third world, Yezirah, is the world of Water.

Yezirah is the world where Time begins; the one where forms exist and definitions can be made. The *idea* of a human comes from Beriah but the different *forms* of human—male, female, black, white, tall, short, stocky, slender etc.—are defined in Yezirah.

It is also the world of mental images, emotions and the human soul. Paradise is in Yezirah and so is hell; they are both psychological, not physical, realities and Kabbalah teaches that we can live in either of them in our essence at any time, whether we are alive or dead.

Finally, there is Assiyah, the World of Earth—where we are physically incarnated to play the Great Game of Life. Although the lowest world appears to be very strong and sturdy to us, it is actually the most fragile of the four. The Earth could be destroyed very easily—that is, the physical Earth. The Yeziratic, Beriatic and Azilutic Earths would still exist. Physical life is easily broken in all life forms; we can be snuffed out with just one wrong footing on a road. However, all great spiritual traditions teach that it is only our physical bodies which die; our souls go on.

In this great Kabbalistic scheme of life, humans are the only beings who have access to all four worlds of Jacob's Ladder. Archangels have access only to the top two, angels only to the middle two and animals only to the bottom two. We humans are made in the image of God and our job is to reflect all that is in creation back to the Source. As we grow, the Divine baby grows. Kabbalah teaches that we are still very, very young and we are not doing quite as badly as some of us may fear.

As you can probably see, Kabbalah is a complicated language for the beginner—and even the expert cannot have too many reminders. Let's start the Work itself with four pivotal essentials that will help you work well with the concepts in this book.

1) When something happens in one of the four worlds, its effects echo through all the others so, it follows that if we heal something at one level, it has a follow-on effect in the others. A change in perception can alter a long-held belief which can change habitual emotional patterns which can heal a body. A physical accident can change thoughts which can change beliefs which can change destiny.

Similarly, each of the sefirot of the Tree of Life is linked to at least three of the others so healing or neglecting just one aspect of life can have a powerful knock-on effect.

We all come into each of our lives with a particular map or destiny to follow, demonstrated by the blueprint shown in our astrological chart. This is not necessarily what modern concepts might deem important such as success or fame, rather it is a plan that is woven in with our soul's development and, in its own infinitely small way, it affects the outcome of all things.

Because of certain choices made by us and by others, that

destiny may be challenged and even changed through what Buddhism calls "unskillfulness" at any level or it may be enhanced and changed for the better by skilful decisions and actions.

We may never know if an accident or an illness was part of our life's planned path or whether it occurred because we were wilful or careless or exposed to harmful toxins. What we can know is that we can heal the thoughts and emotions around what happened and, if we do that, then extraordinary levels of healing can be achieved. It's always wonderful when that healing is physical but a psychological and spiritual healing at a soul level will always lead to a better quality of life even if the body does not recover.

Sometimes there is a deeper purpose in a physical or mental health situation than the ordinary mind can comprehend. Consider the legacies of lives such as Helen Keller, Stephen Hawking, Andrea Bocelli, Marlee Matlin, Jim Carrey, Robin Williams, Brian Wilson, Carrie Fisher or Mark Twain. I realize that is cold comfort if your body hurts or you are in depression or despair over a lack of physical healing but often the resistance to what is, is the pivotal reason why it continues. I hope to show that Kabbalah can help with a deep, inner acceptance that is transformative on all levels.

When I was seriously ill with cancer, I fought and resisted, I worked and studied, I prayed and invoked, I changed diet and lifestyle and it seemed that nothing worked—but in fact they all worked. Each part of the process was a layer of the onion in my healing. But it was only when I surrendered, allowed and released that the physical manifestation of my healing came. It is possible that my physical body will always be weaker than it might have been without the disease but that aspect is nothing compared with the depth of the strengthening of my soul and it can serve me as a continual reminder to be conscious, happy and focused. And, perhaps even more importantly, to appreciate my life every moment that I have it.

2) We live more than once. Reincarnation is accepted in Kabbalistic systems as is the concept of Karma—both good and bad. Many folk say, with justification, that "life isn't fair". Certainly, one life may not appear to be fair.

Dr Daniel J. Benor, founder of The Doctor-Healer Network, taught me that there are four levels of negative karma:

- Pencil on paper—something which can be erased with a simple apology.
- Pen on paper—something which can be erased but will probably leave some scarring.
- Chisel on stone—something which may take another lifetime or even two to repair.
- Blood in stone—true evil which a soul may have to work on healing for many generations.

Karma frequently runs in families and nations because it is the result of repeated patterns. Like astrology, it is what happens to us when we don't use our free will. But free will requires consciousness and we humans are far more comfortable in the egoic, repetitive mind.

We all accrue karma because we are unskilful beings. I have a theory that we get to choose in each lifetime how much good and bad karma we want to use up—it's not just the bad stuff! We often forget the idea of good karma—and it's possible that it could be a lot like credit card bills. You can pay them off slowly or you can choose to do it in one big lump. I'd say that anyone who chooses the latter is a brave soul who deserves our admiration and respect.

We can certainly change quite a lot of negative karma in just one lifetime by amending patterns and performing good deeds.

3) Whatever our problem may be—physical, psychological, financial, emotional—the root cause must be healed for the

issue to be resolved. There may well be a taproot such as genetic illness, an emotional wound, a physical infection or a time of bad fortune which is the obvious issue but dis-ease is always multifaceted and there are many subsidiary roots to heal, too—not least one or more of the four relationships. The healing is always the same journey, whatever the issue. It is the journey of "coming to our senses" and taking what could be called a pilgrimage into our soul and beyond. It is also an individual journey; you have to make your own pilgrimage to find the healing appropriate for your soul and that may take time and effort but it is more than worth it.

4) Grace simply is. Grace has nothing to do with karma, the law of attraction, our concept of God or anything we deserve or aspire to or desire. It deserves its capital letter because it is the attribute of divinity that is all-embracing love.

Grace, however, challenges everything we believe because Grace is kinder than justice and something that is kinder than justice is, to our human minds, radically unfair. We are programmed against Grace.

You can't earn Grace or expect it or understand it but you can allow it or refuse it. It is from Grace that miracles come. And miracles do come. If this book teaches nothing other than the ability to allow Grace, it will have more than achieved its purpose.

Chapter Four

Climbing and Descending the Tree

The easiest way to demonstrate how the Tree of Life works is to climb it. However, climbing it is challenging.

For the purposes of healing, we'll be using the Tree rather than Jacob's Ladder. This is how it develops our first concept of the four relationships as seen in the four central sefirot.

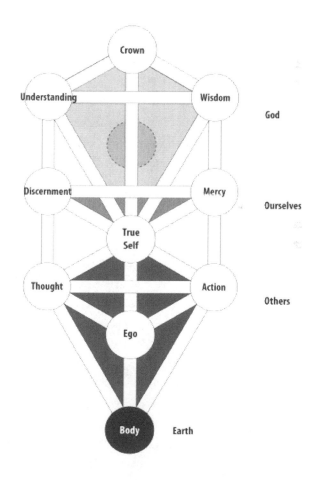

- Trinity/God/Divinity: The upper "kite" of the Tree: Keter, the crown; Binah, understanding; and Hokhmah, inspiration and wisdom; linking to *Tiferet*, truth and beauty.
- Ourselves: *Gevurah*, discernment, strength and discipline; *Hesed*, loving kindness; Tiferet, truth and beauty.
- Others: The lower "kite" of the Tree: Tiferet, truth and beauty; *Nezach*, action, passion; *Hod*, thought, play; and *Yesod*, foundation or ego.
- The Earth: *Malkhut*, the Kingdom.

This is how the average person lives, as reflected on the Tree (and everyone uses this universal pattern in one way or another whether or not they know it). It's a simplistic version as we are all complex and fascinating beings.

1. Malkhut. We perceive the physical reality of a situation.
2. Yesod. We form an opinion of what that situation means to us and our security according to our habits, training and beliefs. This will be a reaction, based on what we've learnt from outside sources and whether it forms a threat or a benefit to us.
3. Hod. We seek more information about that situation or we start discussing that situation with others, sharing similar experiences and seeking more information to support our existing belief. Conflicting information is generally discarded at this level as it doesn't feel good and we believe that it is unlikely to be true.
4. Nezach. We take action based on our beliefs and thoughts giving feedback to Yesod on what did or didn't work.
5. Tiferet. We lock down our opinion of the situation as "my truth". In doing so, we close off to any higher knowledge that might make us think anew or see alternative paths.
6. Gevurah. We judge ourselves and others and other

situations according to our inviolable truth. This is instead of having the strength to discern that all people and all situations are different. We will see others as either right and therefore good, or wrong and therefore bad. Or, conversely, we believe that we, ourselves, are wrong and wicked and we sink into guilt, fear and depression.

7. Hesed. We give time, kindness and attention only according to our judgments—to the sort of people/ situations we believe in. We believe that we give because we are good people but, more often than not, we give in the hope of being appreciated, loved or acknowledged.

8. Binah. We believe that the whole of life—for everybody— is based on the assumptions we have made and our brain becomes able only to receive and transmit the same, repeating message—ensuring that we keep experiencing it in reality.

9. Hokhmah. We are open to dramatic revelations only according to those beliefs. "I knew it!"

10. Keter. We regard God as either a religious rule-maker or non-existent. God is formed totally in our own image and we deny ourselves the opportunity to open our hearts and minds to the new.

Coming down the Tree would work like this:

1. Keter. We are open to the great Oneness of harmony, love and perfection. We may perceive a physical situation but we know that it is only the manifestation in time and place of an old energy and it can be amended at any moment.

2. Hokhmah. We receive inspiration that opens our hearts and minds to new perceptions which lift our hearts and give us a direction.

3. Binah. We create and hold strong boundaries—not

spilling our perceived wisdom to those who may disparage or destroy it—and we realize that we may have inbuilt or taught beliefs that oppose our true guidance. We consider deeply what may have held us back before and commit to healing it.

4. Hesed. We love—unconditionally—all people, including ourselves. We give time and energy to ourselves so we may shine for others. We pray or work to heal where we can, whether or not we approve of, believe or like the other.

5. Gevurah. We discern what is good for us and what is not and where we can help and where we cannot. When we cannot help, we move away to create space for those who can. We discern what is power and what is control. We gently but firmly take steps to ensure that we are where we are meant to be and cut out the dross in our life that may prevent us—and others—from moving forward.

6. Tiferet. We stand strong in our truth—a flexible and loving truth. We hold power and both act and respond with humility. We do not need others to perceive that we are right and we are willing to accept the truths of the other as being valid.

7. Nezach. We take clear, strong action, bringing down all the attributes from higher up the Tree to empower us. We are able to perceive when to start, when to stop and how much energy to expend on our work, play and interactions so that the experience is fulfilling and effective.

8. Hod. We continue to be open to learning new things. We edit or amend, hone or discuss our life, thoughts and actions with God, ourselves and with other like-minded people. We know exactly when to speak and when to be silent.

9. Yesod. We observe that we have built a strong foundation

of helpful and supportive beliefs. We are attracting people who help and advise us and we are perceived to be strong, reliable, clear and prosperous. We also observe the unhelpful and destructive patterns in others with compassion but refuse to allow them to affect us.

10. Malkhut. We manifest true prosperity at every level and know that our life is good.

Now, this may seem like Cloud Cuckoo Land but it is exactly what Jesus meant when he said, "Seek first the Kingdom of God" (Matthew 6:33). Malkhut means "kingdom" and the kingdom Jesus is asking us to attain is the kingdom of Azilut, the Divine world, where everything is in the eternal Now being perpetually recreated. This is also the Keter of the Yeziratic Tree of Life, our own higher self. If we start there, from that very concept, our life can change in a second.

Let's take the analogies a little further. Supposing you have a diagnosis of an acute or chronic disease. This is how it might go from the bottom of the Tree up.

1. Malkhut. There is a serious—maybe critical—disease within our body. That's a fact.

2. Yesod. Our reaction. After the initial shock of denial, all the negative information about that disease rises up and overwhelms us. We feel terror, shock and disconnection. We may believe that our life is destroyed and we are helpless. All of this comes from old information—what we have heard, seen or experienced throughout our life as being reality. We feel paralysed.

3. Hod. We talk with people and research the disease, relying on our existing views of allopathic and/or holistic medicine. We research the existing medical beliefs and the views of those who have already encountered this disease. We read about the details of any available

treatment. If there is a reasonable prognosis, the fear lifts a little but is still liable to hit us hard at times. If we are holistically-minded we may begin to search for alternative ways to help ourselves.

4. Nezach. We start physically doing what we can to help ourselves even if only attending doctors' appointments. If we are naturally exploratory, we may change our diet or start looking for therapists. We may feel hope if we do take action but, if there is no quick turnaround, that hope may be dashed quite swiftly. If we are not naturally exploratory we may stubbornly continue life as it was — or we may take action to put our affairs in order.

5. Tiferet. We start making clearer responses to our treatment — how much we will take into our own hands and what we are willing to undergo of conventional treatment. Or, according to our temperament and training, we simply hand ourselves over to the medical profession and hope for the best/fear the worst. We may join a support group; some of which are helpful and healing but some of which perpetuate the continuation of the illness by enabling us to make it part of our actual identity.

6. Gevurah. We make decisions — or not — and we may experience blame and guilt and start working with these deep emotions or feel overwhelmed by them. At this level, it is either totally our own fault or totally someone else's that we are sick. This is also the level where an allopathic treatment may remove the disease, which is wonderful. But without a strong Gevurah to change our life and practices, it is likely that the disease — or another one — will return in the future.

7. Hesed. If symptoms have gone, we may begin campaigning to raise money for charities to do with our disease in the hope that others do not have to suffer as we

have. If the symptoms have not gone, we may begin to seek sympathy or pity for our situation and live our life from the perspective of the illness — whether it is currently manifest or not. We may discover that this disease gives us power over other people for the first time in our life and we may take comfort from being admired, respected and loved for the stance we have taken and wonder why we never stood up like this before.

If we have recovered, we may not climb any higher on the Tree at this point as there is no necessity; we can return to our everyday life—unless we have chosen to be an activist. If the latter, we may become somewhat of a fundamentalist about our new belief. If we have not recovered, the journey continues.

8. Binah. We settle into life as a wounded or diseased — or campaigning — person and expect others to behave in the same way, accordingly. We will be unlikely to access any deeper understanding of Binah.

9. Hokhmah. We reject all new ideas that may help us heal, outright, because this is now our identity.

10. Keter. We become our disease and our soul begins to fade even if our body continues for a long time.

N.B. All disease is potentially healable up until the point of death as demonstrated by stories such as the miraculous recovery of Anita Moorjani, author of *Dying To Be Me* (Hay House). Reading about somebody's last-minute, miraculous turnaround may not be overly helpful if we are seeking healing earlier in the journey but the message of the book is about transforming the relationship with ourselves through self-love and that is of tremendous value.

Here's how the journey of healing may go from the top down:

1. Keter. We are lifted out of our everyday psyche by the shock of diagnosis and suddenly realize how valuable life is, that the world is sacred and beautiful and feel an incredible joy that overpowers the fear.

2. Hokhmah. We find every day to be a miracle. We are able to say that the diagnosis has changed our life and we are eager to work with the knowledge we are receiving from above and from our body.

3. Binah. We understand that time, boundaries, decisions and relationships must be reassessed and reworked as now is all there is and it is incredibly precious.

4. Hesed. We love. We love the world, its people, our family, seeing all as One ... and we may embark on our bucket list or on an incredible adventure that changes us so radically that we forget to be ill.

5. Gevurah. We decide to cut out the dead wood, change our diet, change perspectives that are no longer useful, embark on the discipline of self-help, therapy or treatment. We may even walk away from our family, realizing that our relationships have been toxic. We work consciously with any treatment we have.

6. Tiferet. We discover where any death wish may be within ourselves and either heal it or accept it with peace.

7. Nezach. We embrace a new lifestyle, whether physically or emotionally or both.

8. Hod. We assess our progress and adjust accordingly.

9. Yesod. We accept—even know—that all is well.

10. Malkhut. We heal.

It must be said here that there are also those who start at the top of the Tree, at Keter, and become completely disconnected from reality. They can dive into delusion, going off on their own flights of fantasy which bring no good results whatsoever—but that's when they are only connected to one side of the Tree and can't balance themselves.

There are those who feel all the wonderful emotions above and know that this is the appropriate time to die so it is even more important to clear out the negatives. They are the ones who die consciously and are a much-needed example to all of us. Everyone has to die eventually and it is an incredible gift to the world to die consciously and wisely.

And there are also those at the bottom of the Tree who, through sheer dogged persistence, clear all the debris as they climb up. We are all different but the basic analogy still stands.

For the experienced Kabbalist, the path up or down is simpler because the levels of the Tree are better understood. To attain Keter, the knowledgeable would go into meditation and lift his or her consciousness above the physical reality and the ego's fretting directly to Tiferet, which is the place in the psyche that is connected directly to spirit, then through the "black hole" of Da'at (inner knowledge), to the Divine in order to access Grace.

But for the rest of us, this would be the healthy journey of healing up the Tree.

1. Malkhut. We acknowledge that there is a dis-ease in some form and that we cannot continue as we were; something must change.

2. Yesod. We stop lying to ourselves about the dis-ease, we own it as ours and we cease blaming others for it. We take responsibility (ability to respond, not blame) for it. This is our dis-ease and we are the only ones who can heal it through our thoughts, choices and actions. If we are lucky, it is something that can be "cured" by allopathic medicine but, if that is the case, it is also likely that without inner work the dis-ease or an equivalent one will appear again in the future because it still has something to teach us.

3. Hod. We stop treating our body or our problem as a thing

and we cease allowing others to treat us as things. A thing can be fixed; a human must heal on several levels; a dis-eased human is a soul who has lost connection somewhere with its own health and truth. We research alternatives.

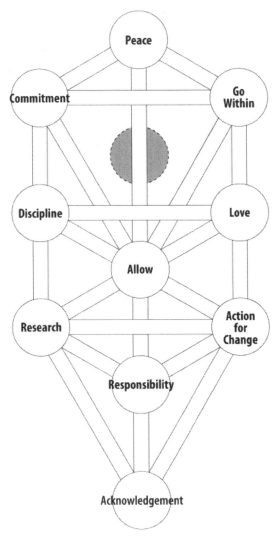

4. Nezach. We stop poisoning ourselves. It may be as simple as changing diet because we need more or different

nutrients but the reason why we have the desire and the need for the unhealthy food must also be addressed. We need to examine which thoughts and beliefs are also poisoning us. It doesn't matter how right we may be about those thoughts and beliefs, it is still those which are hurting us, not the external situation that prompted them.

Each of us has our own poisons and many of them are cunningly hidden, such as addiction to social media or caffeine or sugar. They always feel good when we have our hit and it hurts when we deny them to ourselves. The development of self-discipline is always a challenge, especially when previous external discipline has been inadequate or too harsh.

5. Tiferet. We allow hopes and dreams to live instead of squashing them. Life force is a form of creativity and all humans must be creative in order to be happy. It doesn't matter if creativity is being able to dress yourself beautifully, bake a cake, paint a picture, write a song or a story, plant and tend a window box, raise a child or build a cairn of stones on a hill. The moment we stop singing, dancing, creating or looking for new experiences, we begin to starve our soul. Yes, you may say, but "they" stopped me. They may well have stopped you but you can start anew. Sometimes it's as simple as noticing when you stop caring about your appearance. Of course it doesn't matter if you wear old clothes, clothes from the charity shop or things that don't match; what matters is whether your clothes are clean and how you feel when you wear them and whether you still take care of your body.

This includes supporting the hopes and dreams of others instead of squashing them—no matter how ridiculous they may seem to us. It is all too easy to say,

"Oh, that's been done!" or "You'll never make it!" or "That's a stupid idea," but this is a form of psychological murder. A word of kindness is incredibly powerful.

6. Gevurah. We embrace the discipline of accepting that change is necessary for healing. This requires strength, discernment and courage and it is possibly the greatest challenge. We move away from family, friends and situations that are preventing our healing.

    We also stop over-giving and overdoing and develop a healthy selfishness. It is now time for us, not time to be a doormat.

7. Hesed. We realize that the only true answer is love. We love the world, the moment, nature and life itself. All too often, this requires forgiveness — and forgiveness is anathema to the ego; after all, if they did you wrong then they are the bad one and you are the good one, right? The ego really, really wants to hold on to that one.

    But forgiveness has nothing to do with the other and everything to do with you. For the longer we hold on to a hurt, the longer it hurts us. The other will probably have moved on to a happy life. That doesn't mean you don't rant and rave and complain; just that you don't keep on and on and on ranting and raving and complaining. You start retraining your mind to look at all the good there is in life and appreciate the kindnesses that you have been given.

    The best revenge is to live a happy life.

8. Binah. We understand that our commitment to our own healing is not selfish but a gift to the world. The more we can learn and do to be a person of peace, the more we serve the greater good. As Elizabeth Gilbert wrote in Eat, Pray, Love (Penguin): "All the sorrow and trouble of this world is caused by unhappy people. Not only in the big global Hitler-'n'-Stalin picture, but also on the smallest

personal level... Clearing out all your misery gets you out of the way. You cease being an obstacle, not only to yourself but to anyone else. Only then are you free to serve and enjoy other people."

9. Hokhmah. We become still, we may meditate. We open our hearts and minds to inspiration and allow guidance (which will frequently seem off-the-wall to start with) to come through and teach us the way forward.

10. Keter. We are at peace with God, whatever we perceive It to be.

As you can see, climbing the Tree requires huge effort and discipline and, if we don't trust what's at the top (God), then we are simply not going to do it.

That is why the first healing we have to do is with our relationship with the Divine. If we can't do that, we are unlikely even to begin the rest of our pilgrimage to health.

Part Two

Our Relationship with the Divine

Chapter Five

The God Issue

Let's pause here for a moment for a few words about religion.

Religion is what we humans have used to justify cutting ourselves off from Unity. It is not God's fault; it is ours.

The root of the word religion is thought to come from *ligare,* the Latin for "to bind". Ideally, "re-ligion", from *religio*, means to bind back together or to reconnect. Good religion is the kind that closes the gap between you and other people and God, so that the illusion of separation disappears. "Bad" religion—which is what most of the world experiences—binds you to the rules and ends up separating us from others and from God.

That the root of the word comes from Latin is appropriate; it was the Roman Empire which created the God that most of us in the Christian world worship, despise or disbelieve. Before Rome (and its predecessor, the Greek Empire) religion wasn't a *thing.* It was part of the Whole; an element of life. Our connection with the Universe and Nature had no name, it just was. Yes, there were names for specific gods, ceremonies or groups but they were all just different aspects of the One. As the writer with the pseudonym *Philologos* writes on the Jewish *Forward.com* website, "these were discrete things; religion itself was the unnamed totality of them all, the forest that couldn't be seen for all its trees."

That began to change, in Judaism, about 500 years before the birth of Jesus, with the coming of the Second Temple where the earlier, more inclusive methods of worship were discarded and law became the focus rather than the Whole. The early Christians created a hiatus from that with a simple faith that welcomed the outsider, the woman, the slave; one that taught of a great Love that would hold us in our suffering and resurrect us (whether we died or not) into its all-embracing compassion. But when Christianity was adopted by the Roman Empire, the political dance began again and the specifics of what was the "right" way to worship and what was the "wrong" way were decreed. Christianity was putty in the hands of the Emperor Constantine who transformed it into a suit of armour of Righteousness. And there it has been ever since, inspiring all other religions to do the same.

"To bind" or "to re-bind" can be voluntary or involuntary. It *can* mean to commit yourself to something good but binding that good still carries the danger of removing all possibility of growth, flow and updating. Kabbalistic teaching is that the Perennial Tradition *must* be updated for each generation or it will wither and die.

The majority of what we believe about God is not conscious but conditioning. Whether or not we actually believe in the God that our religion or culture purports to be the real one, we are imbued with the cultural understanding of generations within our society. Even atheists are affected by what has been ingrained in their psyches and, generally, atheists and mystics disbelieve in almost exactly the same God—the punitive one who could, but won't, stop cancer or wars. The only difference is that mystics have developed the will and the discipline to enter into a personal relationship with the Divine and understand Its bond with them and the Universe while atheists are perfectly content to do without. I would venture to suggest that many atheists are far more in touch with true divinity than many religious folk.

I would sum up religion as being a container for the ego and/or the child within us. When we are starting out on our exploration of spirituality it is good to have guidelines and a supportive tribe. However, as we grow, we are meant to outrun that religious vessel and develop our own direct contact with the Divine. Christianity does teach this with the tearing of the veil in the Temple at Jesus' death (Luke 23:45). Only the high priest could move through the veil but, without it, we have direct access to God.

However, hatred of religion—no matter how negative it may have been—will not help our healing. Rather, it will oppose it. Religion's problems are always caused by adherence to law rather than openness to spirit, tribal patterns and in refusing to update.

It is always better to shine a light than to curse the darkness and through understanding the Perennial Wisdom and living our lives as an example of the light, we can offer a safe pathway out of the trials of religion for those who want one.

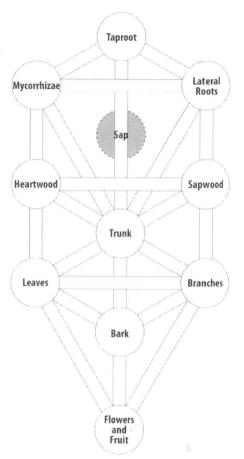

The Tree as a Tree

If we consider the Tree of Life as having its roots in the Divine, then it will help us to understand how important this foundation of a clear and strong connection with God is. Without strong roots, nothing can thrive.

Let's take a brief detour here to show how the Tree of Life—as a real tree—demonstrates this beautifully.

Keter: Radical or Taproot

All germinating seeds have a taproot, the primary life-giving root which heads straight down into the soil and provides the nutrients and strength for growth. Taproots require fertile, moist and well aerated soils and, in many trees, may become damaged quite early on. The tree's continuing growth and strength then depends upon the lateral roots which take over for the rest of its life. Keter is the source of all Grace and life force.

Hokhmah: Lateral Roots

Lateral roots become far more important to a tree as it grows and in many cases replace the taproot. As we will see when we examine the side triads of the Tree of Life, this is the equivalent to religion replacing direct contact with the Divine. The lateral roots spread out along the surface of the soil, rarely going deep into the ground. This is only a problem if the ground is infertile or external conditions challenging.

Binah: Mycorrhizae

Mycorrhizae are fungi which grow on root systems taking sugars from plants in exchange for moisture and nutrients gathered from the soil by the fungal strands. They greatly increase the tree's ability to absorb vital nutrients such as phosphorous and act as extensions to the root system. Neither fungi nor trees could survive in most uncultivated areas without this mutually-beneficial arrangement. Mycorrhizae also give protection against disease.

The use of fertilisers both disrupts and replaces these fungi in gardens and cultivated areas.

Da'at: Sap

Sap is the blood of a tree, carrying its vital life force of nutrients and minerals. Its level of flow depends on the seasons, with it being most active in springtime. Like Da'at, the healthy flow of sap is internal, a direct line of communication between source and being.

Hesed: Sapwood

All wood starts as sapwood. It is formed just under the bark by a thin layer of living cells known as the cambium, which produces bark cells to the outside and wood cells to the inside. Tree stems increase in girth during each year of growth because a new layer of wood cells is added inside the cambium. Sapwood is living and physiologically active. In young trees and young parts of older trees, all of the wood in the stem is sapwood. But as the tree gets older and its trunk increases in diameter, things change. No longer is the entire cross-section of the trunk needed for conducting sap.

Gevurah: Heartwood

This is older sapwood which alters to change function as the tree ages. It is technically dead but it is the strength and support of the tree as well as being filled with resins and minerals which protect the whole structure.

Tiferet: Trunk

The inner trunk of the tree, or cambium, is the growing part of the trunk. It creates both sapwood and a substance called phloem which processes and carries photosynthesised nutrients from the leaves. It is the melding point of all the tree's inner constituents and its centre or heart space.

Nezach: Branches

The purpose of branches is to spread as wide or high as possible in order to gather sunlight for photosynthesis. They also spread the area where seeds may drop and attract nesting birds to eat and spread their seeds.

Hod: Leaves

Leaves absorb light through their chlorophyll pigments and the absorption of carbon dioxide via their stomatal pores. Through the process known as photosynthesis they both feed the plant and release oxygen into the atmosphere.

Yesod: Bark

The outer bark is the protective covering of the tree. It is also what we first perceive when we look at it—just like Yesod is our persona presented to the world in order to attract what we need and keep us safe.

Malkhut: Flowers and Fruit

Flowers and fruit are the end result and crowning glory of the tree. It is here, at Malkhut, that the end result of all the processes of the other sefirot are revealed in manifestation. "By their fruits shall you know them" (Matthew 7:6). However, these are the most delicate aspect of the whole structure.

Making God in Our Image

Each of the Trees of Life in Jacob's Ladder are made up from two kite shapes and four side triads. In Yezirah, where we humans live mentally and emotionally, the top kite shape of Keter, Hokhmah, Tiferet and Binah (Source, inspiration, truth and understanding) also forms the bottom kite of Beriah, the spiritual world and touches the Divine World of Azilut (see figure on page 35). This kite would be our spiritual heart and lungs, inhaling inspiration and what Eastern faiths call chi.

The Keter of Yezirah is the Malkhut (Hebrew for "kingdom") of the Divine World; the place Jesus called "the Kingdom of God". It is also the Tiferet of the Beriatic, spiritual world and when all three aspects of this sefira are activated through human consciousness, it is the conduit of the miracles that are consistently present in Azilut. A miracle is simply the opening of one world to another.

This upper Yeziratic kite is the level of Being where our psyche may be imbued with Spirit or our Spirit may be discounted or rejected by our psyche. Whichever it is, this is the aspect of us which experiences direct contact with Universal forces and, combined with the soul triad of Tiferet, Gevurah, Hesed (truth, discernment and loving kindness), processes—or rejects—everything new that we experience.

Astrologically, this kite is represented by the fire sign of Leo; here, it is about dominion over our own life and acknowledging our own divine kingship—coming into the Kingdom of God. However, negative Leo can be prideful and certain that it is right, overruling any possible greater truth and will try to establish its own kingdom of rulership on Earth.

The bottom kite of Tiferet, Nezach, Malkhut and Hod (truth, action, physicality and thought) is also the top kite of Assiyah, the physical world, and this level of being is in direct contact with our body and either drives or is driven by the physical world. You could think of it as the digestive and excretory system. This lower part is involved with everything in our lives that repeats itself.

Tiferet is the linking point between the two kites and it is both the seat of consciousness and the seat of our soul. It is only at Tiferet or above that we have access to free will; every aspect of our psyche below it runs on programming as do the four side triads connected to it.

Most of us believe that we take conscious decisions much of the time but probably 95% of our decisions are based on previous experience or reactions to external stimuli. A decision taken from Tiferet often feels noticeably different from any other and frequently it may feel uncomfortable because it is new. It can also be challenging to maintain any new decision in the face of social opposition. The majority of our psyche is devoted to comfort or, at the very least, the devil it knows and, in most humans, Yesod, the ego, rules the true self, Tiferet, because the part of our psyche that gets used the most becomes the strongest. But if we want anything in our life to change for the better, it has to be the other way around. That takes effort and discipline.

The lower kite is represented by the astrological sign of Cancer. Cancer is the "mother sign" of caring and open generosity towards all. But a crab depends on its outer shell for protection and has no backbone so it can be very defensive and needs strong boundaries. Negative Cancer over-gives and requires a return of love and acknowledgment—and will attack anything it perceives might breach its defences.

To show how mired in we are to the lower kite of Yezirah, I often ask people to change simple habits such as cleaning their teeth or putting their clothes on in a different order—or even crossing their arms the other way around. None of those are easy or comfortable things to do and both our body and ego will resist them; the change just feels wrong. Understanding this is an important step in healing. Our egos and bodies don't want to try anything new unless it automatically feels good which is one reason why allopathic medicine is so popular; take a drug and feel better. Bingo! No need to do anything yourself that might feel uncomfortable.

Being Centred

When we are balanced, focused and centred in Tiferet, we can observe our habits and behaviours and make clear decisions as to whether they are helpful ones. We can experience anything new consciously, note our reactions to it and make an informed decision based on the information and knowledge we have. We can perceive the powerful influence of Spirit and may be a conduit of Grace. The black hole in the Tree of Life, known as Da'at, is the link point—what I call the cat flap—between our psyches and direct contact with the Divine. It will open either way so, if we are open to new influences while being centred, we receive Grace, inspiration and guidance. If we are not open to the new, the flap is only opened from below as we project our lower psyche up into the centre of the spiritual world of

Beriah, creating automatic replays of our previous experiences to unfold. That's how the Law of Attraction works. Whether our lower psyche is happy and balanced or depressed and angry, we will request more similar experiences through Da'at into Beriah which answers with like-to-like. Because we are children of the Universal creative force, we are creators. We can either do it consciously or unconsciously.

It is never our fault if we are doing this in a negative way, unconsciously; it is all to do with our programming and beliefs. But once we come to realize that we are the creators of our reality then we become responsible. We have the Ability to Respond or rethink. We can either think anew or think the same. Persistent new thought carries the guarantee of change; persistent old fault unravels yet more of the weave of our life.

Inspiration comes from Keter, via Hokhmah and Binah to Tiferet or straight down through Da'at to Tiferet. You can tell the difference because the first is a flash of insight followed by a feeling of acceptance or rejection and can be overthought or neglected and forgotten. The second is like waking up, refreshed with renewed life force and an "oh, of course!" feeling. The reason for the difference is in the programming of the side triads. In a baby, these triads are clear; the child simply loves and desires to explore and play. Distress is momentary and generally from physical discomfort. Concepts such as what is right or wrong are learned later; no baby is racist or homophobic or hates in any way. But as we grow, we develop neural pathways in the brain that become our automatic programming. By the time we are seven years old, the programmes in the side triads become so hard-wired that we have virtually no awareness of their existence. This is of vital importance if we are to understand our relationship with God.

Principles

The ego is at Yesod and is like Da'at in that it is a window or cat flap between worlds. This one communicates between our psyche and our body and is the seat of our gut feeling. It is programmed by repeated patterns and has no concept of whether something is morally or ethically right or wrong; something is good simply if it pleases us, makes us feel safe or satisfied; something is bad if it threatens us or gives us discomfort. The intellectual side triads hold us to higher standards—or at least, that's the idea.

The side triads are programmed according to whether we focus our attention on the upper or the lower kite of the Tree of Life. As a child we are open to mystery and magic but we are frequently taught to look down rather than up and, as a result, we will draw our tribal beliefs into spaces originally intended for wonder.

Ideally, as babies, we experience caring parents, often holding their loving gaze and believing that we are one with all we experience. The first shock of separation, that we are not one, is the first forming of the ego. It learns the concept of "me" and "you" and, with skilful parenting, this experience is one of excitement and curiosity. With unskilful parenting it is the beginning of fear.

Our second shock of separation is our "acceptable" and "unacceptable" self. The ego truly believes that if its needs are not met we will die and, to a certain extent, it is right. Our brains are programmed to learn very swiftly as to what behaviour gets attention from the "others" which is beneficial to us (i.e. feeds us and keeps us warm) and what behaviour doesn't.

We will either conform to the acceptable or rebel against it. However, the early formation of the rebel attitude is usually just another way of getting the attention the ego needs. In a large family, the parents will be more aware of the difficult child than the good child.

Our third shock of separation is mind from body and soul. This is when we are taught definitively to trust outer authority rather than our instincts and intuition. This is the death knell for a healthy Tiferet or relationship with the Divine and the time when the intellectual side triads of ethics and morality start to become overloaded.

Our fourth shock of separation is the concept of life and death. We either experience this through the deaths of animals and relatives or we are shielded from it and only perceive its possible existence through books and television. A child that only understands death as a fictional device or one who is told that there is nothing after death will not find it easy to cope with the shock of loss or grief, nor to open up to the spiritual world. It is only through admitting that we do not know all the answers that we will seek Grace for ourselves.

It cannot be overemphasised how powerful early childhood is in the make-up of our psychological Tree. When exploration and new experiences are not encouraged and when wonder, awe and magic are not present in a young person's life, there is no healthy development of consciousness at Tiferet so Yesod rules the roost and God becomes a programmed concept. And when repeated patterns become the norm, they filter from Yesod up through the triads and paths, unquestioned by an unconscious Tiferet, to become beliefs and emotions that are set in stone.

Recovery from this programmed, rational mind requires a re-centring that is opposed by today's busy, entertainment-filled society at every level. The ego will always try to look for a distraction from its pain rather than experiencing it.

It generally takes a major shock, an illness, a tragedy or a miracle to bring us back to full consciousness. Fortunately (though we won't see it that way) at least one of those wake-up calls is virtually inescapable during life on Earth.

Chapter Six

The Side Triads of Intellect and Principle

The side triads are formed by our repeated thoughts and intellect. They are what Sigmund Freud referred to as the Super Ego and the Super Ego Ideal. These differ from the lower ego at Yesod because they are about convictions and thoughts, whereas Yesod is about communication between psyche and body and about feelings and safety. The top triads could be defined as what I think/don't think, believe/don't believe *about God and others* and Yesod as what others feel/don't feel about *me* and how I experience that. Yesod is our gut feeling; it is very personal.

The intellectual side triads define our ethical and moral beliefs, our philosophy and principles and the kind of God we believe in, assuming that we believe in one at all. We are dealing with them now because if we don't understand the power that they have over us, it is unlikely that much else in our healing can be achieved.

It is always challenging to define ethics and morals. "Ethics" comes from the ancient Greek word *ethikos*, derived from *ethos*, which means custom or habit. The Roman politician and lawyer Cicero used the term *moralis* as a Latin equivalent of ethikos so the roots of the words "ethics" and "morality" do, essentially, mean the same thing.

However, for the purpose of these triads, I'm defining ethics as what we believe to be right or wrong and morality as what we do with that knowledge. I would also suggest that ethics are the rules provided by society and law and morals are the actions decreed by our religion or belief system. These triads dictate our approval or non-approval of pretty much everything!

Integrity (central column) is what we will have if our ethics match our morality.

- A balanced left-hand triad does the thing right. Its ethos is fairness.
- A balanced right-hand triad does the right thing. Its ethos is justice.

It may be fair to jail for life someone who has killed a fellow human but, depending on the situation, it may not be justice.

Positive discrimination may be justice but may also be unfair.

As you can see, this is a potential minefield.

The super ego is the rules and regulations we believe that society should live by: eat your greens; wear clean underwear; believe in this God; tell the truth; recycle your rubbish; spend religious festivals with your family; don't rock the boat—and many more.

The super ego ideal is how we live our lives in relation to those rules—positively in the aspect of inspiring or helping others less fortunate than ourselves, negatively as seeing ourselves as being somehow exempt from them because we are special or know better. We may believe we are special because of the God we believe in or through narcissistic belief that we are above the rules and regulations that govern others. It is the Super Ego Ideal that colonises other countries for their own good; believes in the divine right of kings or the power of the military to change the world.

Neither side triad will be aware of, nor care deeply about, any distress it may cause because it is right and "if the other could only see clearly, they would understand that."

What we believe in these side triads dictates our lives without our realizing it. Carl Jung taught that 90% of our energy—both good and bad—resides in the unconscious.

Both Jesus of Nazareth and St Paul refer to this hidden matter as yeast. It is good yeast if we are living a happy, "risen" life and harmful yeast if it eats away at our soul. As St Paul writes in 1 Corinthians 5:7, we must "throw out the old yeast and make ourselves into a totally new batch of bread." He is using the metaphor of the old yeast for our patterns of negativity and contentiousness, which we must bring to consciousness to heal.

Our patterns of belief are very localised. For example, in the UK we may learn that it is fine for the cuddly lamb we are encouraged to pet to become roast lamb for our dinner but it is not fine for the beautiful horse we see and are encouraged to ride to be served up in the same way. In France, the latter is perfectly acceptable. This is why new experiences such as travel are so important for us; it is Yesod, the lower ego, that automatically rejects foreign ideas or foods as "other" and prefers to revisit the same holiday or same kind of holiday because that feels safe. It is Tiferet which will venture somewhere new and different to discover the new. If we consistently seek the new and are willing to learn about it, we have to use our Tiferet especially if it leads to the shock of a realization of other realities rather than what we have believed to be true. If we use this realization then we can reprogramme the side triads.

Ideally, realization leads to discernment and compassion (Gevurah and Hesed). But when the side triads are seriously overprogrammed so that our beliefs are so strong that they will not accept an alternative view, we will almost certainly lean towards blindness and fundamentalism.

Another example of how the side triads operate would be the example that Buddhists are vegetarian and yet Tibetan Buddhists frequently eat meat—the elevation and climate of Tibet makes an arable society virtually impossible. It is forbidden in their religion to kill an animal to eat but they are permitted to eat meat killed by Muslims. Is that hypocrisy or simple pragmatism? The loading of your side triads will judge that one for you.

Someone who perceives cruelty to animals in the food industry may turn vegetarian or vegan, becoming passionate about their belief and encouraging others to change too. This only becomes fundamentalism when they dismiss the idea that others may have the right to a different belief. All they may see is that they are right and the others are wrong and cruel. They will have ethics on their side but they will have no concept that they are holding themselves superior to those with other beliefs. The superiority game is one that the super ego ideal just loves to play.

It gets more complex with a situation such as fox hunting. To a farmer whose lambs are being taken by foxes and whose livelihood depends on raising and selling them for food and whose only alternative is to patrol a dozen or more fields with a gun at lambing time, the idea of a hunt might be both ethical and moral. However, this stance may not be perceived by a city dweller or someone who is not a farmer or who is an animal rights campaigner.

To a meat-eater, who has no concept of the farmer's life, or to a vegetarian, a hunt may be both unethical and immoral. The first would be through the concept that the fox is innocent and inedible and the second because those responsible for the killing of it are having fun while doing it. There is a modern moral outrage at the idea that a human should enjoy killing of any kind—for the most sensitive of us it is hard even to pull up a vegetable! However, 90% of us would experience a sense of satisfaction in killing a mosquito that wanted to drink our blood and we gorge ourselves on films and television which feature horrific violence without a second thought—because we are, obviously, on the side of the "good guys" which makes it all perfectly all right.

The only emotions the intellectual side triads work with are fiery. Passionate belief is marvellous if positive but its negative is anger. The more watery emotions—love, sentiment, sympathy, guilt, grief and pain—are focused in the lower triads either side of Tiferet. Side-triad anger is "righteous anger" based on a belief of superiority—and all the more dangerous for that. It is all about what "the other" should or should not be doing because what *we* are doing is right. It is righteous anger that gets the crucifixions done.

These intellectual side triads pierce the soul triad of Gevurah, Hesed, Tiferet (discernment, loving kindness and truth) and, if they are over-primed they will engulf the soul, leading to judgment and imposed "truths" without the option of clarity or compassion. Adolph Hitler and the Nazis were certainly working from over-fuelled intellectual side triads to be able to send Jews, Gypsies, homosexuals and other people their programmed beliefs judged to be inhuman to the death camps.

The Arab-Israeli war is also a conflict of these side triads. The Zionist view is the principle that as God gave Abraham "all the land that you can see," then Israel has the right, and the only right, to inhabit that physical area and the temple must be rebuilt in Jerusalem, even if it means killing others and destroying their property. However, the mystical, Kabbalistic, view of God's message would be that Abraham was being told that he would receive all that he could perceive which, at that time, included the physical land. However, the mystic, experiencing divinity through the top kite of the Tree of Life, would be willing to see that the dream of a sacred homeland was primarily an inner experience. Jesus tries to clarify this for a people groaning under the yoke of the Romans, who also want their land back, "Neither shall they say, Lo, here! Or Lo, there! For, behold, the kingdom of God is within you" (Luke 17:21).

Without a clear relationship with the Divine we cannot understand a foundational teaching from both the Hebrew and New Testaments that all our needs will be met. Instead, Arabs and Israelis, who are essentially cousins, believe that their livelihood and their religious faith are reliant on the external possession of land. Both sides are being destroyed by belief that the other is wrong and the inability to allow God to intercede with good for both. This is entirely understandable because the great mystical truths have been untaught or discounted for so long and we believe so powerfully that we have to control matters ourselves.

If you want to know whether you are acting from an imbalanced side triad all you have to do is check out whether you feel superior or inferior to somebody else when you consider your ethical, religious or moral stance on something. As the world becomes more law-led, religious, atheistic, and increasingly convinced that we are the ones in control and less connected to the Earth, most of us feel superior about something.

The Left Hand Triad

The left-hand triad of Binah, Tiferet and Gevurah (understanding, truth, discernment) is restrictive; a valuable balance to the

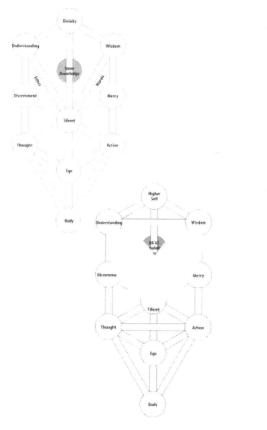

right-hand triad of Tiferet, Hokhmah and Hesed but, if overemphasised, rigidly negative. These are the mycorrhizae that support our life. Beliefs here are intellectual and judgmental. This is the accounts or legal department of life and the ritualised aspect of the scientific mind. It works doggedly to the rules. In a seemingly trivial example, in my husband's family, the rules were that you always finished up the top layer of a box of chocolates before eating any from the layer below. In my family, my parents preferred the hard centres and were happy for us children to go to the second layer for the creams before they had finished the top layer. It initially shocked my husband the first time that I changed layers without even thinking because his programming saw greed where mine saw normal practice. We had to discuss our families' rules quite extensively before he could be at all comfortable with my behaviour. Now he is more flexible and I am just slightly more restrained in order to match comfort zones. Take this example to the wider world on what is accepted practice (e.g. arranged marriages, religious laws, ethical practice, law etc.) and you can see huge causes of conflict not because the beliefs are "true" but because they are wired into our brains.

This triad either legislates in an attempt to make the world a fair and equal place—or to keep aspects of the world "in its place" according to the policies of the country, company or judiciary ruling body. It regulates medicines, groups and societies to ensure they practise according to specific standards. It cannot countenance a holistic medicine such as homeopathy which cannot be tested by the scientific method nor accept that a something which works on spirit or soul rather than directly on the physical could be of any benefit.

It is also the triad of your religious laws, politics, national characteristics, such as the British stiff upper lip, and of nationalism: "My country, right or wrong."

This triad is represented by the astrological sign of Aries, which may seem strange as the god Ares (Greek)/Mars (Roman) is associated with warriors, but his original role was as god of agriculture, a strategist for when was best to sow, weed and harvest a crop and both defending and protecting his land. It was only after we created fences around land and countries that Ares/Mars became a god of war.

Positive Aries is strategic, courageous and determined and willing to listen to different points of view. Negative Aries fire will dismiss or strike down a foe (a rival opinion) without a second thought. It may even attack when there is no quantifiable threat.

The Right Hand Triad

The right-hand Intellectual Triad, Hokhmah, Hesed, Tiferet (inspiration, mercy, truth) is the one that rules the concepts that we have about whether or not there is a God, whether the Universe is benign or malignant and whether there's a heaven or a hell. These are the lateral roots that so often take over from the direct contact of the taproot.

Beliefs here are intellectual but exciting because both Hokhmah and Hesed are the epitome of enthusiasm. If we rebel against these beliefs, we will believe ourselves to be inspirational radicals in a world of pedants and if our beliefs are fundamentalist, we will have a need to proselytise them. When this triad is locked deeply into the "rightness" of a belief, it will feed pride into Tiferet. Pride is the soul's kryptonite. While it's absolutely fine to feel proud of a job well done, a beautiful thing created or a good idea, to feel proud of the rightness of your beliefs of your nation or your religion will always become a destructive force that leads to hatred and the despising of others.

This is the triad of the missionary, the innovator, the Inquisition and the *pogroms*. In balance, it brings genuine good news of goodwill and it fuels exploration and discovery. Out of balance its concept of mercy is savage. It will attempt to save souls by killing people or it will eradicate a race because it is perceived to be inhuman. It is the manifestation of corporate greed that cares nothing for the planet and of Big Pharma which purchases health services to make a profit.

Here there is no need for guilt or self-analysis or sorrow, for it can all too comfortably be translated into blame. This is the place where you can simultaneously not believe in any God but still hit out against It. When this triad is negative, it can only see a deity that appears to be willing to fix the minister's car but can't be bothered with cancer or a holocaust.

In our own lives it is often revealed through passive aggression, particularly on the Internet where it is safe to attack others. Memes such as "90% won't re-post this but I know my real friends will" are classic demonstrations of the projections of this level of consciousness.

This triad is represented by the astrological sign of Sagittarius. Positive Sagittarius is the generous philosopher, the liberal, focused on justice, travel, expansion. Negative Sagittarius is a complete hardliner when it comes to its liberality and is unable to hear facts or deal with people that oppose what it believes to be true. It is also tactless, careless and impatient.

The Truth?

The good news about both these triads is their proximity to the central triad of Binah, Hokhmah and Tiferet (understanding, inspiration, truth) which means that a dramatic experience or revelation from Spirit or the profound shock of a wake-up call can and will transform our learned beliefs and judgments into new insights. The bad news is that nothing in these side triads is Truth with a capital T. They are what we think is truth. Whatever we observe or learn will be coloured by what we think about it and what we think about what we think about it—layer upon layer of projection. What is True, with a capital T, is the Perennial Truth, it always has been true and always will be true;

it is not a cultural, emotional or intellectual belief or what we have learnt to believe. Those are illusions. Our moral stance will almost always make us instinctively avoid the concept of a greater Truth. For example, there's a comment on one of my YouTube videos about Kabbalah that says, "Women can't learn or teach Kabbalah." This is posted underneath a video of a woman who is quite clearly teaching Kabbalah. In his culture and belief system women are not allowed to teach Kabbalah and therefore I cannot be teaching it. Any evidence that contradicts this is therefore not allowable.

When overblown, the side triads are the part of us that believes that we own the truth. No one owns truth — the second we believe we own it, we have lost it. They can and will block our access to spirit, leading to rigid concepts that avoid the conscious holding and awakening aspects of Tiferet. When this blockage is created, it transmits information down the side pathways of the Tree of Life from Gevurah to Hod and from Hesed to Nezach. This means they programme our lower ego and our body, bypassing our conscious knowledge and becoming beliefs at the survival level — to be fought over tribe-to-tribe as a method of survival.

The primary harmful illusions stored in the intellectual side triads are those concerning:

- God
- Religion
- Authority
- Money
- Government
- Royalty
- Moral Superiority
- Race
- Sexuality
- Gender

As all three upper triads are represented by fire signs, we have to use fire to heal fire. Fire is the element of the divine world of Azilut and it is to heal these side triads that we have to reassess our relationship with God. You'll have heard the term "the healing fires of Grace". Grace is always available to us—it cannot be earned, it just is. We simply have to open our hearts and minds to accept it.

If we don't do that first then we will use any negative beliefs we might have about divinity or religion to scupper all other attempts to start our healing. Deep-held concepts such as God not caring about us, not thinking we are worthy, wanting to punish us for past errors or not allowing us to be both spiritual and wealthy are like fire extinguishers to Grace. Whether it's unconscious, subconscious or conscious, if we carry one iota of any of those, or other negative beliefs about God, we will self-sabotage every step of the way—even to the extent of allowing hope and evidence of a new start and then scuppering it in a way that is so devastating that we dare not try again.

Chapter Seven

In the Beginning

The spiritual teacher, Byron Katie, says that if you hate anyone, then you cannot love God. That is worth reading over and over again and digesting. Certainly, one of the best ways of working out whether or not we have a clear relationship with the Divine is to assess whether we believe that God hates the same people that we do.

We'll know if we have an issue with God if we are sure about what God is or isn't. That's because the opposite of faith is certainty. Religion is usually sure; our intellectual side triads are always sure. Both are rational, social, verbal, linear or transactional. Faith is mysterious, receptive, transformative and always open to the new. Faith is being present, now. That's unpredictable which is why so many people avoid it, preferring the often outdated written word.

If we aren't at peace with God, we cannot be at peace with ourselves, our emotions, our bodies or our finances. Kabbalah teaches that we are all atoms in the body of God's divine baby, vital and integral parts of the Universe. Mystical Christianity calls this divine baby Christ—something that has been in existence from the beginning of time, personified in a bright and brief encounter with Jesus of Nazareth—and in others too. Judaism calls it Adam Kadmon. In essence we are part of God, so being uncomfortable about God is being uncomfortable with our own essence—our source point—and it is a serious blocker to Grace. The moment we consider God as being something totally external to ourselves we will falter, close off our contact with spirit and rely on—and expand—the beliefs in the intellectual side triads.

It's absolutely fine to be an atheist; just not an anti-theist.

An anti-theist is one who is angry about the idea of God and has to protest the absence of Divinity. Anti-theists are often fundamentalists, projecting huge anger. Any long-held anger and resentment damages our soul and our spirit, whether or not we believe we have either. All fundamentalism comes from the side triads.

Some of the most peaceful and powerful people I know are atheists. They take responsibility for their lives on Earth because they believe that nothing is going to rescue or condemn them and they get to choose good instead of being driven to it.

Some of the most angry and unhappy people I know are religious. They have lost contact with spirit because of their adherence to law and tribal religion and demand that everybody else should change to fit their criteria of what is right.

Most of us live somewhere in between, often believing that we are at peace with our concept of God when we are not. Spiritual folk often hedge this whole issue, calling God "The Universe" or "Source Energy" and that's all well and good if their lives are happy and prosperous. If their lives are neither then they are still being affected by negative side triads and avoiding the root issue. It is quite understandable that the word "God" has all kinds of connections with patriarchy, cruelty, abuse and control but it is exactly those concepts that we need to clear rather than covering them up or avoiding them with another name.

Over several decades, I've found that unacknowledged anger with or fear of either God—or our concept of God—is a major cause of poverty; certainly in the Western world. God is the source of all supply and if we don't clear our root resentments with religion or our beliefs about being unworthy, we can be as spiritual as we like but we will never be prosperous. Money is a neutral energy force and is constantly imbued with our thoughts and feelings. As it is the modern "source of all" then it reflects our inner faith exactly.

Without a deep inner knowledge that we are one with All and

that the All is the natural flow of abundance, we believe that we have to struggle and suffer in order to prosper. Many holistic teachers say, "Do what you love and the money will come," but I never found that to be the case until I had cleared my own inner demons about God. Only then did I discover what I truly loved to be and do rather than what I *thought* I wanted to be and do.

Finding the Root

To heal the wounds in and around God, we have to find the source of the loading in our side triads which, for most folk raised in the Western world, is religious interpretation of the Bible. These teachings have permeated society for generations, also affecting those not of the Abrahamic faiths and, although we now live in a far more secular world than ever before, they are still, effectively, written into those side triads.

Let us start again.

"In the beginning, the Elohim created the heavens and the Earth."

These are the first words of the Book of Genesis. The word *Elohim* is translated throughout the Hebrew Bible as "God" and there is, nowadays, fierce debate amongst scholars as to whether it is masculine or feminine. Every single word in Hebrew comes from a root made up from three consonants and, before the Hebrew Testament was set in stone after the destruction of the Second Temple in 70 CE, none of the Biblical texts included any vowels at all. So each root word was a picture which could have many meanings. And, as there is now only one version of the formalized Hebrew text available, we have no idea of what the first words intended were.

What we do have is an agenda about it. Every single human being has an agenda about God.

Mine is that God does not have an agenda about us.

What is clear to the Kabbalist is that the whole process of creation as described in the Bible is a Divine dance between masculine and feminine held together by the unity of the One.

It would appear that the root of Elohim, the letters *lamed, he, mem* in Hebrew, could be masculine if translated with an "e" at the beginning or feminine if translated with an "a". It is generally agreed that it is a plural noun rather than a singular one, that Ruach Elohim, "the spirit of God" in the second verse of Genesis, is feminine and that *Yahweh*, the accepted name of God, is non-gendered and a verb rather than a noun, having the meaning of "To Be Being". Yahweh, by the way, only shows up with the creation of humanity and then only as Yahweh Elohim. Yahweh alone is only mentioned after the exit from Eden.

My Kabbalistic colleague, Hebrew scholar Stephen Pope, author of *Patterns of Creation* (Axis Mundi) says that Elohim simply cannot be fully translated but interpretations of it include movement, stillness, breath and mother waters.

Elohim made humanity after Its own image: "male and female created S/He them both" (Genesis 1:27), which means that any Biblical translation of God being wholly masculine is pretty much out of the window whichever agenda you may have. Yes, Jesus calls God *Abba* or Father but we don't need to set that in stone. *Amma* or Mother is just as appropriate.

So, we might reasonably deduce that nearly all Biblical translation is inaccurate and that the original probably orally-transmitted story may well have been non-binary and inclusive.

We can also conceive the idea of Trinity—and not just in the Christian sense. Trinity is the relationship between unity and diversity, the Cosmic Dance of the Source and the Divine Masculine and the Divine Feminine as depicted in the top three sefirot of the Tree of Life.

It begins with the concept of creation (Keter) leading to the spark of creation (Hokhmah) which is nurtured in the womb of creation (Binah). This would be the dance between Elohim (God), Yahweh (the Lord) and Ruach Elohim (the Holy Spirit).

This concept of God was not some invisible deity that required our belief or worship but the great unity of patterns within and behind the whole Universe. Despite the crystallisation of religion through the great empires, Wisdom Traditions such as Kabbalah have always held that God is unknowable except through direct experience—and that the Divine is impossible to define, let alone explain.

At the root of the whole of the Perennial Tradition is the idea of clearing old, unhelpful beliefs from our hearts and minds so that divine love can flow into our conscious Self. That glory then fills us to the brim so we can heal in depth and inspire others do the same.

It's my experience that we can retrain our intellectual side triads with the intellect. But, if we do, they will only *behave* better, rather than being totally transformed. What's more, it's a long job of affirmation and mind-reprogramming and the resistance from our brain can be very powerful. Each programmed belief has already formed an electronic neural pathway in our brain— long-held ones form actual physical pathways according to Deepak Chopra's *Quantum Healing* (Random House)—which is like a computer programme. Our brain will run that belief until that pathway has been reprogrammed with a better one and falls into disuse. Even then, our brain may default to the previous pathway at times of crisis.

This makes the discipline of using affirmations for long enough to rewire the brain a challenge, especially if we are holding hundreds of negative beliefs about God, ourselves and others.

However, if we focus on clearing the issues around God first, allowing Grace to flow into our psyche, we will be experiencing a transformative force which gives us strength and conviction and, most importantly, powerful back-up to get the work done.

Grace
Grace is a helpful word to embrace on our healing journey as

every definition of spiritual Grace defines it as something which cannot be earned. It is the giving of clarity, kindness, love and healing as a blessing. Grace can be compared with chi because it is life force itself but the essence of it is that it is a power to transform negativity into the positive. You cannot be unworthy of Grace; Grace is always present on the central column of consciousness and always available if we will simply open the door to her.

Grace is defined in St Paul's letter to the Romans as being the antithesis of law. Grace cuts straight through all those side-triad beliefs and approvals to give us relief. Romans 6:14 (my translation) says: "For harmful thoughts shall not have control over you: for you are not subject to law, but held within Grace."

Many of us, on beginning spiritual work, have experienced miracles. Perhaps a sudden flow of prosperity, a relief from symptoms, a surge of love. We are inspired and happy but the feeling doesn't last because the old beliefs and approvals regain their power. The answer to that is to invoke Grace daily, perhaps even hourly, to ensure that we are directing it to help our healing. If we don't direct it, experience tells me that it becomes diverted to our habitual neural pathways in the form of chi or life force, making them stronger. Directed, it enhances and speeds up our healing.

When our world is coloured by illusion, which the side triads are, it's almost impossible to discover your true self, let alone love it. The Prayer of Grace in chapter ten draws the purity of Divine Love down through the Tree of Life so that we are restored and revealed, gently and slowly in our true beauty. To invite Grace into our whole psyche daily is the most powerful intent to heal that we can have. It is a glorious practice and, if you can find the discipline to do it, it will make the following intellectual and emotional work so much easier.

Chapter Eight

The Jealous God

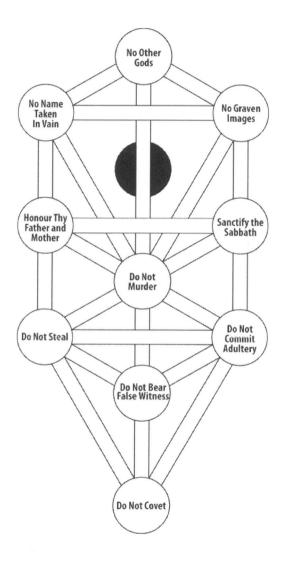

Now that we understand how tangled our beliefs can be, we can begin to unravel them. The best way for our brain to handle this with respect to our relationship with God is to go back to the first laying down of the law in the Abrahamic traditions. As it would most likely have been versions of the Bible teachings which caused any problem in the first place, that is the best place to start with the healing. It doesn't matter whether or not our consciousness thinks the teachings are rubbish, without a radical reinterpretation all that will be added to them is anger or resentment. Both of which, ironically, make them stronger because we may even come to need their existence in order to be self-righteous about rejecting them. Reinterpreting, updating and re-weaving these texts through the sefirot means we are using the same loom. Our brains will find that easier than starting all over again.

The First Commandment

I am the Lord thy God, which have brought thee out of the land of Egypt, out of the house of bondage. Thou shalt have no other gods before me (Exodus 20:2).

On the Tree of Life, this commandment is placed at Keter, the place of our higher self, our crown chakra and our access point to the Divine. As the Malkhut of the Divine world of Azilut it is also "the Kingdom of God".

The phrase "the Lord thy God" is Yahweh Elohim, the "everyday" name for the Ultimate Name that is given to Moses at the Burning Bush. The Ultimate Name is *Eheyeh Asher Eheyeh*, generally translated as I Am That I Am. Scholars tend to emphasise that it is more I Will Be What I Will Be but either works because Hebrew is a pictorial language with limited tenses. The essence is all about Being.

This is the ultimate definition of the clear relationship between the human and the Divine. For the mystic, it is an expression of God the Transcendent and God the Immanent: God manifesting in and through us. God is to you what you will be to God. Even more than that, because God and Creation are one, you are God. You are simultaneously God and in relationship with God. This is the great mystery that the intellect will never understand; it can only be experienced.

God is all that is. God is all that is happening at every moment. There is no "mind of God" for God is all consciousness. God is not a being, or even a Supreme Being, but Being itself. Each of us is a weaver of the I AM in our own place and time. God can only manifest through us to the extent that our free will allows It to do so.

This means that we are a vital part of this whole creation journey; living, breathing, moving images of God whether we know it or care about it or not. "I was a Treasure unknown and I desired to be known so I created a creation to which I made Myself known; then they knew Me," says the *Hadith Qudsi*, the Islamic collection of the direct words of God. The Treasure is the whole of creation and the knowing of it is you.

Most scholars and religious folk will tell you that the Name of God is Yahweh and that the Elohim part is almost incidental. But the Book of Genesis makes it clear that it was the Elohim who created the Universe, not Yahweh. Yahweh turns up as consort only with the creation of humanity and Yahweh Elohim describes the meld of masculine and feminine divinity in One with the advent of gender in the story itself. It is only after the "fall" of Adam and Eve from Eden (Yezirah, where their psyches were formed) to Earth (Assiyah, where they became actual physical beings) that Yahweh takes supremacy and becomes perceived to be male—and Temple Theology[1] teaches that much of that may be due to judicious editing of the Bible after the fall of the First Temple when the worship of the Divine Feminine was forbidden. Until that, She had equal place with Yahweh in the Temple itself and it is likely that they were viewed as masculine and feminine aspects of the One rather than male and female gods.

Kabbalah will take the mystery deeper, understanding that

none of the names of the Divine are truly translatable. As we saw earlier, Elohim can mean "movement, stillness, breath" and "mother waters" and my colleague, Stephen Pope, translates Yahweh as "to be Being". Neither is the war-mongering, judgmental Lord we have been taught.

It was a revelation to me in reading the Bible with a Hebrew companion to see how often humanity's wars and desecrations came about because we simply ignored a wise and guiding word from one of the aspects of God. Chapter Eight of the first book of Samuel is a good example. When the prophet is nearing the end of his life, his people ask him to ask the Lord (Yahweh) for a king to rule them.

This is the Lord's reply:

This is what the king who will reign over you will claim as his rights: He will take your sons and make them serve with his chariots and horses, and they will run in front of his chariots. Some he will assign to be commanders of thousands and commanders of fifties, and others to plough his ground and reap his harvest, and still others to make weapons of war and equipment for his chariots. He will take your daughters to be perfumers and cooks and bakers. He will take the best of your fields and vineyards and olive groves and give them to his attendants. He will take a tenth of your grain and of your vintage and give it to his officials and attendants. Your male and female servants and the best of your cattle and donkeys he will take for his own use. He will take a tenth of your flocks, and you yourselves will become his slaves (1 Samuel 8:11–17).

But the people won't listen and it is from their decision that all the following Biblical wars and destruction come.

If you read the Hebrew Testament of the Bible in the original language you will also see that the Holy One is referred to by many different names and in several different, subtle ways throughout and it is perfectly clear in that there is a tapestry of masculine and feminine working together, indicating the facets (the sefirot) of the Divine and attempting to guide us accordingly. Generations of scribes have slashed the tapestry of this great Teaching, probably not deliberately; more likely because they didn't know the oral teaching that underpins it.

Mystically, this first commandment states simply that we need to put our spiritual growth and understanding before anything else. It is not "you must worship God" but "you will thrive if you seek connection with the Ultimate Oneness of All Things which is also within you".

The commandment also makes it clear that there are other gods; a god being whatever it is that those side triads of ours worship or revere. In the modern world we prioritize many things before our spiritual connection. Our "gods" include money, power, family, partners, sex, celebrity gossip, pets, sport, social media and religion, not to mention being right.

True spiritual connection is always non-dual; it sees truth in all things and can be summed up in the phrase "yes and..." rather than, "yes but..."

At the level of Keter, we have the clarity of the eagle, able to soar above and see the wider picture rather than focusing down on the minutiae. And we do not blame. It's fair to say that most of us get there rarely and, when we do, it is only briefly.

"The house of bondage" in the commandment refers to the Israelites' years of slavery in the land of Egypt. In the Book of Exodus, Moses was sent to free them and take them on the physical and psychological journey through the wilderness to the Promised Land. This whole story—like many in the Hebrew Testament—is a metaphor about how to release ourselves from thought-forms of slavery and enable us to lift our hearts and minds to freedom.

I've known people who preferred to focus on the mention of Egypt in order to argue that the Egyptian pantheon of gods is wonderful and this is a prejudicial story. The secret, if that troubles you, is to replace the word "Egypt" with whatever has you enslaved. Simply spending 24 hours practising not believing anything to be right or wrong can be hugely revealing of the power of our unconscious programming.

The Divine world doesn't judge, it just IS. We, and our human-made religions, are the judgmental ones.

Kabbalah teaches that the healing lesson at this level is to let go of all habits, prejudices and beliefs. That is a colossal undertaking which is why most folk, quite understandably, don't begin their healing journey at this level. And yet, if we don't begin here, we won't clear the pathways that can give us so much strength and guidance in every other aspect that we desire to heal.

Many of us don't love God at all because of hard religious teachings or bad experiences with ministers. But the simple truth is that if you don't have a God you can love, then you have an inaccurate God, one that was taught to you, not experienced directly. It is more than worth the time and effort to explore the idea of an all-loving Divinity that you can trust and put first in your life. I know from experience that this is a magical journey of healing at all levels.

For many of us, the block has been the idea of Jesus being God—and an exclusive God at that. This is also an inaccuracy from the programming of the religious side triad.

Jesus Christ and Christ Jesus

There is so much misunderstanding about Jesus and Christ and God. Contrary to popular opinion, Jesus is not referred to as God in the New Testament. He is referred to as Lord. The one exception is when the disciple Thomas says, "My Lord and my God," when he has put his finger in Jesus' wounds and I think, given the circumstances, he can be excused...

People in Biblical days would have understood the difference between the two; we don't. Lord in lower case in Hebrew is

Adonai, LORD in upper case refers to Yahweh. Adonai is the name and aspect of God placed at the sefira at the Malkhut of the divine world of Azilut. So Jesus could be an aspect of God—a gatekeeper—but *never* the whole of God.

This sefira is also the Tiferet of Beriah and the Keter of Yezirah and is representative of the crown chakra. It is no coincidence that also Keter means crown. This is a hollow crown, through which the Divine flows into creation. Jesus, during his life on Earth, embodied this presence and his injunction to us to follow him is to encourage us to reach that level in ourselves as well. Note that Jesus never once asked us to worship him, only to follow him. St Paul does call on us to worship but to worship Christ Jesus, not Jesus Christ. The wording is significant. Christ Jesus is the Christ Consciousness which manifested one time on Earth in Jesus but was present from the beginning of creation and is still existent and present without him. Jesus Christ is the human who embodied that consciousness as an example to us.

Do you get the subtle, yet vital difference? As the wonderful Franciscan, Father Richard Rohr, says, "Christ is not Jesus' surname."

As Christ, Jesus demonstrated a human access point to the Divine. Whether or not you believe in the divinity of Jesus is actually not all that important. Christ itself exists as one-third of Trinity. The Divine is all three aspects of Trinity—Source, Christ and Holy Spirit. So, effectively, it is blasphemous to call Jesus, alone, "God."

In Kabbalah, Adam Kadmon is the Cosmic Christ. And as the Cosmic Christ, It is the presence of God that can become a physical being at any time in any world. John is the Gospel representing the Divine world of Azilut and in this Gospel— the one with all the great "I Am" sayings—Jesus is speaking as the voice of the Cosmic Christ, not as the human man. When he says, "I Am the way, the truth and the life," he is saying that this aspect of the Cosmic Christ is the way, the truth and the life.

Not one of us will pass into Azilut except through that level of consciousness—through the gateway of the Malkhut of Azilut. Christ is much bigger than just Jesus. Christ is in all humanity—and beyond. Christ is all creation. Christ is not and cannot be limited to one religion. That alone is life-changing knowledge.

Understanding this helps to makes it clear that the Christ is the great potential in all beings. Christ is in the very air we breathe and the food we eat. When we take communion we are acknowledging the sacred—the body and blood—of the Cosmic Christ. And we become what we eat.

Kabbalah teaches that it is our purpose in creation to become perfected—to become Christ. This may take many hundreds of thousands of years—or even more—but it will happen eventually and for all of us. No one will be left behind and, if there are billions and billions of us, Christed, all going, "Come *on*, Fred!" then God will still wait patiently for Fred to make his/her own mind up.

Supernal Triad

We've already taken a good look at the two intellectual side triads which can block our contact with the Divine but the upper kite of the Tree between them must be our focus if we want to re-understand God. The kite has two triads, the Supernal Triad of Keter, Hokhmah, Binah (divinity, inspiration, understanding) and the spiritual triad of Binah, Hokhmah, Tiferet (understanding, inspiration, truth).

The Supernal Triad is the first indication of Trinity. It is the source of a continual flow of Grace in which God the Unity (Keter), God the Father (Hokhmah) and God the Mother (Binah) perform the divine dance of creation. Each flows effortlessly into the other, giving and receiving in full equality. What is vital about Trinity is that the meld of all three is what makes up God. It is never just one aspect.

It is no coincidence that there are three commandments

concerning our relationship with God and each dances with the others. It is also important to note that Trinity is ever-changing, ever fluid. It can be Father, Mother, Spirit or Source, Christ, Spirit—and probably many other terms for the same indescribable concept as well. It is flow, movement, a definition of the non-dual. A great, Cosmic Yes, And...

If you look at this triad on Jacob's Ladder (page 35), you will see that Keter is simultaneously the Tiferet of the spiritual world of Beriah and the Malkhut of the divine world of Azilut. Even that one sefira is both one and many, on three separate levels.

Where the triad beneath comes into play is the connecting (or not) with human free will. The flow of these three divine dancers creates a fourth dancer—you, at Tiferet. At all points, you are involved in this circle of Grace—if you will allow yourself to be so. Da'at can either act as a translucent window or a closed mirror. It can reflect your own image as one of the partnership or show you as being totally separate.

If this is all just getting too complicated, just breathe, relax and know that all we really need to know is that when we choose to take part in the dance, through meditation or contemplation or in experiencing any kind of joy, we are channels of Grace. When we close our hearts to it, we see God only as a reflection of our own closed-off psyche and in the forms of rule-led religion.

Silence, symbols, poetry, music, dance and sacraments are much more helpful than words in experiencing Trinity because it is ultimately inexplicable: beyond our concept of existence. As Joseph Campbell, the American mythologist, once said, "We cannot conceive of God, let alone think about God, let alone speak about God."

Christians often think that Trinity is unique to their faith but there is plenty of evidence of it in the Hebrew Testament. Research into the design of the first temple shows the Holy of Holies (Keter) together with the pillar of Yahweh (Hokhmah) and the pillar of Ashratah/Elohim (Binah) in the sanctuary.

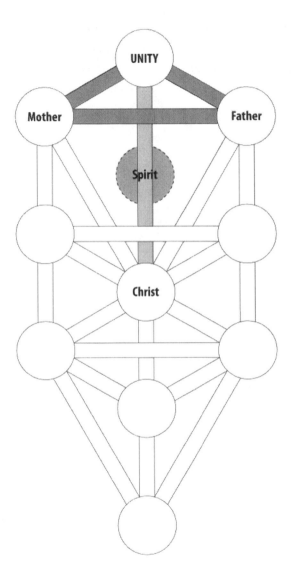

In sacred literature, the Divine Feminine is both mother and bride of the Lord... the wife of the Lord gives birth to a son and becomes the mother of the next Lord. And yes, that works just as well for all genders, e.g. the partner of the One becomes the parent of the next One. And in the wisdom literature of the

Book of Job, when Job himself sees and experiences God directly instead of perceiving It as the Other, he is given seven sons and three daughters. The sons represent the seven lower sefirot of the Tree. Only Job's daughters are named and the meanings of their names define the three sefirot of the Supernal Triad.

"The first daughter he named Jemimah (living in the moment—Keter), the second Keziah (empowering breath—Hokhmah) and the third Keren-Happuch (splendour of light—Binah)" (Job 42:14).

The mystical Christian view of Trinity is just as beautiful though it is a different interpretation from the one of the Supernal Triad. In this tradition, Keter is the Divine, Da'at is the Holy Spirit and Tiferet is the Christ.

It is generally spoken of as "God the Father, God the Son and God the Holy Spirit" but Christ Itself has no gender, even if Jesus did. After Rome took over Christianity, we forgot that the message Jesus brought was that we too would do and be as he was as long as we looked up into the womb of the Divine to the Source and joined in with the dance. That's exactly how all of us find peace with God.

The upper kite of the Tree of Life is represented by the astrological sign of Leo. Leo is the king, the wise, benign ruler who represents the Divine on Earth. However, if infected with spiritual pride (the Tiferet of Beriah) the king is despotic and cruel. Jesus' Beatitude "blessed are the poor in spirit" refers to the importance of holding balance in the Tiferet of Yezirah (the Malkhut of Beriah) rather than laying down the law from an arrogant spirit.

Chapter Nine

The Graven Image and the I Am

The Second Commandment: Hokhmah

Thou shalt not make unto thee any graven image, or any likeness
[of any thing] that is in heaven above, or in the earth beneath, or in
the water under the earth:
  Thou shalt not bow down thyself to them, nor serve them: for
I the Lord thy God am a jealous God, visiting the iniquity of the
fathers upon the children unto the third and fourth [generation] of
them that hate me (Exodus 20:4).

The words in parentheses are ones that have been edited in
for centuries, allegedly to make more sense of the text. This
is always an issue with the Bible; it has so many edits and
additions from so many later translations and opinions that it is
a great challenge to know what was originally meant. If you are
a Hebrew or Greek scholar, you can spot the changes in writing
style but for most of us it can be a bit of a minefield.

Hokhmah means inspiration, revelation and wisdom in
Hebrew. This is our right brain, the part of us that is intuitive,
innovative and handles spatial information and visual
comprehension.

A graven image is something that is set in stone and therefore
is stuck. It cannot be a part of any divine dance. Ultra-orthodox
interpretations take this commandment as meaning you may not
draw or paint anything living in heaven or Earth. But we are
creators and children of the Creator and it is natural for us to
draw and paint and create things. The commandment is against
making that humanly-created image the only image. Christian
art has broken this commandment for centuries with an image

of God as the bearded old man in the sky being presented as the definitive view of the Divine and also by making Jesus a white man. The Sistine Chapel may be wonderful art but it is appalling theology.

To break this commandment is the antithesis of both inspiration and wisdom. Hokhmah exemplifies the eternal "now" with new insights flowing continually.

These need to be new insights and not the same insights repeating themselves and simply presenting in new packaging. However, most religions slide from the sefira itself into the intellectual side triad of moral superiority. They do this partly by writing down the teachings and refusing to let them update in any way and also by holding to old revelation as if it were new.

Kabbalah teaches that to listen to the words of priests instead of investigating for ourselves is also a graven image rather than true religion. The Koran backs this up: (17:36) "You shall not accept any information, unless you verify it for yourself. I have given you the hearing, the eyesight, and the brain, and you are responsible for using them." But, of course, it is much easier to accept what we are taught as being the one right way because that makes us, and our companions, the ones who are right and therefore superior.

If you have one image of something which is acceptable it means that nothing else is and that leads to intolerance, hatred and prejudice. It's a minefield for the soul and a paradise for the ego.

A strong example of a graven image is the Kennel Club which prescribes exactly how a pedigree dog must look and move to be accepted at show level. Yes, that encourages beauty and it has led to years of intense breeding to precise specifications which ended up with King Charles spaniels in chronic pain through having skulls too small to contain their brains, bulldogs that can barely breathe, many breeds with failing hips and legs and many other horrific results.

In spiritual work there can be a lot of graven images. Even in Kabbalah, it has become a graven image that it may only be studied by Jewish men aged over 40. This is an injunction that many don't realize was only set in stone in the mid-17th century, at the time of the "false messiah" Shabbetai Zevi.

All religions end up as graven images if they work from ideas set in stone. Examples of these in the Bible are St Paul's alleged diatribes against homosexuality in Romans 1 and again in 1 Corinthians 6 and 1 Timothy 1. If you actually read the Greek, he is speaking out against excessive lust, self-seeking desires, sexual abuses and exploitation. He is also most likely commenting on the Roman custom of using male rape as a form of subjugation or humiliation. There is nothing about loving one-to-one relationships in there and yet his words are used as a hammer against all homosexuality. St Paul also makes gossip equally as culpable but no one has ever seemed to notice that one. Jesus had nothing at all to say on the subject of homosexuality.

The second part of the commandment is equally as contentious. The word for "jealous" is *kannaw* which can also be translated as "zealous" or "diligent". This, to the mystic, is indicative of the law of karma. If you lay down the law to others, the law will be laid down to you and so it is decreed that the severity of our actions will rebound back on us.

The word "generation" does not exist in the Hebrew and it is generally accepted by scholars that it was added to try and make sense of the sentence. Mystics agree that this is possibly a reference to reincarnation (a common belief in ancient days) so that the same soul reaps what it sows.

However, the final conundrum is the phrase "of them that hate me," which is another careless translation. The Stone Edition (seen as the definitive translation of the Torah and the Prophets) says, "Who visits the sin of fathers upon children to the third and fourth generations for My enemies."

Their interpretation suggests that the commandment refers to children who take on the behaviour patterns of their parents, while knowing them to be wrong (Sanhedrin 27b). This, it argues, is more virulent than the sin of the parents, because it legitimises such behaviour as "culture", making it into a new way of life and a new set of values—again, programming the intellectual side triads. In Judaism, a child is not held responsible for sins that s/he did not know were wrong. Therefore the commandment does not contradict the Talmudic maxim that children are not punished for sins they did not commit.

There is one more possible translation which is that the Hebrew word used, pronounced *sawney*, can mean to reject or distance yourself from something. This indicates that if we remove ourselves from the Divine, we are more likely to subject ourselves to the lower laws of karma. Karma, by the way, is far more "that which is like itself is drawn to itself" or "what goes around, comes around" than necessarily being given a hard life because you were badly behaved in the previous one.

Very often, however, we don't even know what healthy or diseased patterns we are holding; they may have been imprinted into our genetic structure without our even realizing it. And that is why the phrase "let go and let God" can be so frightening for us; we simply don't know what we would be letting go of—and our graven image is not necessarily of a loving God who will replace it with peace, happiness or health.

Set patterns can only be changed when we bring them to consciousness.

Finally, the giving of the last set of the Ten "Advisements" itself appears to break its own commandment as they are set on stone. That, itself, is a message to those opening up to the heart of faith to look deeper into the story and understand that if we seek God ourselves, we will be able to download the oral, continually updating "law" of love.

In Kabbalistic astrology, Hokhmah is represented by the

planet Uranus, the bringer of revelation and revolution. Uranus changes things dramatically and suddenly—like the smashing of the sapphire commandments—breaking through our illusions and making us start again. However, for all that the planet brings revolution, it is always the same revolution. Look at the overcoming of Tsarist rule in Russia in the early 20th century. It was replaced by a regime at least as limiting and set in stone in its precepts. Nearly all military coups, changes of governments and new monarchies are greeted with great hope and excitement by their supporters but the system remains and rebuilds the same structure. Without the balance of its companion sefira of Binah, Hokhmah will refuse to learn from its mistakes and patterns and will jump again, and again, into the same situation.

The Third Commandment: Binah

Thou shalt not take the name of the Lord thy God in vain; for the Lord will not hold him guiltless that taketh his name in vain (Exodus 20:7).

A better translation for the Hebrew word *naqah* than "guiltless" might be "clear" or "pure".

Binah is the sefira of understanding. This is not the dissemination of information but deep contemplative understanding of the meanings within the teaching. It is also the sefira of the left brain in humans, our rational, logical and objective selves, handling language and logic. Ideally this is the root of understanding, that we can observe, select and comprehend in depth. It is also the place of clear and sound boundaries. However, when our training is more interested in being right than being happy, we can be led from intellect and rules instead of our souls.

This commandment is about the Ultimate Name which is given to Moses in the Book of Exodus, 3:13–15: I Am That I Am or I Will Be That Which I Will Be.

For the mystic this refers to God the Transcendent: the Absolute All... and God the Immanent—the part within us that is also Divine. As children of God we are creative partners with the One which means that every time we say, "I Am," we are calling down power.

The great Hebrew statement of faith, "*Hear, O Israel, the Lord our God, the Lord is one,*" (Deuteronomy 6:4) states just that. It is sometimes a stretch of faith to get here but it means that everything seemingly separate is all part of the One, just like a drop of water is an integral part of the ocean. Therefore one drop of water that contains poison or one that contains joy will affect the whole ocean.

All Jesus' seven great pronouncements, including "*I am the way, the truth and the life*" (John 14:6), are in the Gospel of John which is the Gospel of the Divine—of the world of Azilut (Matthew is the Gospel of Assiyah, Mark the Gospel of Yezirah and Luke the Gospel of Beriah).[2] They reflect this great unified I Am. In every one he repeats, "I am, I am," at the beginning, although this is never translated from the Greek. The words are *ego eimi*, referring to both the transcendent and the immanent. He is calling the Divine into himself as we all can do. He is not demonstrating that we can't get to God except through Jesus; he is affirming the power of the Divine working through someone who has access to this level of consciousness—the Christ Consciousness. No one can get to Azilut without passing through the sefira of Keter, which represents Christ, but we can all get there whether or not we have heard of, or worship, Jesus of Nazareth.

So to take the ultimate Name of God in vain would not be to blaspheme as in saying "oh my God!" but to misuse the phrases "I Am" or "I will be."

To say "I am stupid; I am unworthy; I am no good" or "I will be hopeless at that" is to take the name of God in vain. You are a spark of divinity incarnate; your every word is a command to the Universe. It affects everything in your life and everything in the life of the Universe.

This is why healing affirmations are powerful, especially the ones which begin with "I am".

However, the affirmative aspect of I Am can also be used very negatively in excluding others. The moment we feel the need to say, "I am a Christian," "I am an atheist," "I am an environmentalist," "I am a vegan," we both affirm superiority and begin to exclude those who are not the same as us. You only have to look at the diversity of species, let alone of humans—race, colour, size, features and character—to see that God isn't interested in recreating the same again and again. God loves diversity but a negative Binah doesn't.

It is also about not using the name of God for worthless things or for vanity—not invoking God to create things which are not appropriate for you or for others. The Hebrew word for "take" is *nacah* which also means "lift up" so the commandment is not to lift up the name of God for dishonest or empty means.

So, don't go to synagogue, temple or church for form's sake only. Don't simply recite learnt formulae when you pray. These kinds of prayer are the form dictated and practised by the intellectual side triads and they simply reconfirm our existing beliefs without opening us up to Grace. They do not dance...

It is also taking the divine name in vain to do any evil in the name of God; or to cause any injury or violence against others in any cause of so-called righteousness. Therefore any holy text that calls for holocaust, jihad or the destruction of anyone in God's name is breaking this commandment.

In Kabbalistic astrology, Binah is the sefira represented by the planet Saturn, which rules old age, bones, boundaries and structure. Saturn is often, falsely, called a malefic planet because its effects wear away customs and habits that we may be comfortable with but which are ultimately harmful to our soul. Hokhmah (Uranus) needs Binah (Saturn) to wear away the repeating patterns that appear exciting but are actually set in stone so that the deeper truth can be seen. Binah needs Hokhmah to bring revelation to our learned concepts, rather like the forest fire that is needed for the seeds in the cones of the eucalyptus, among other trees, to be released.

If just one side sefira is unformed, blocked or damaged, the opposite one, and the intellectual triad leading from it, will run unchecked. If both are compromised, then the side triads will most likely block the central column of consciousness, blocking our ability to receive Grace.

Chapter Ten

Healing our Relationship with God

The Prayer of Grace

This is a way of drawing the healing fire of Grace down through our psyche and body. It opens us up to something far bigger and more benevolent than our concepts of religion.

We start by making the Tree of Life with our body.

Malkhut. Begin by standing with your feet slightly apart and leaning down as if you are going to touch your toes. Just relax and let your torso hang loosely. It's fine just to reach down as far as your knees.

Yesod. Stand up in a relaxed way with your hands clasped below your stomach at your gonadic area.

Hod. Sway on to your left foot and maintain your weight there.

Nezach. Sway on to your right foot and maintain your weight there.

Tiferet. Stand up straight and tall with hands linked at your solar plexus.

Gevurah. Extend your left arm out at shoulder level, with the palm down and keeping your right hand on your solar plexus.

Hesed. Extend your right arm out at shoulder level, with the palm down and keeping the left arm at the Gevurah position.

Da'at. Raise your head to look upwards and turn your palms up.

Binah. Raise your left arm about 45 degrees keeping right arm at Hesed.

Hokhmah. Raise your right arm about 45 degrees, keeping left arm at Binah, so you are making a vessel.

Keter. Put your hands together in the prayer position above your head.

You can then choose whether to say The Prayer of Grace while doing the reverse movements with your body down the Tree or you can simply draw your hands down over your head as though putting on a crown and then down to Tiferet, back in the prayer position and say the words in that position.

Going down the Tree through the Lightning Flash

Begin with your hands in the Keter position, looking upwards.

Hokhmah. Lower your right arm, keeping the left arm at Keter.

Binah. Lower your left arm, keeping the right arm at Hokhmah.

Da'at. Lower your head to face straight forward. Some folk like to draw their hands together at the throat chakra.

Hesed. Lower your right arm to the level of your crown, with palm facing up.

Gevurah. Lower your left arm, keeping your right arm at Hesed, palm up.

Tiferet. Draw both arms in to link at the solar plexus.

Nezach. Lean on to your right foot, keeping your hands at Tiferet.

Hod. Lean on to your left foot, keeping your hands at Tiferet.

Yesod. Lower your hands to below your stomach.

Malkhut. Bend down from the hips to relax your body and ground it.

Words:

From Thee Comes All Grace.
Grace for Connection,
Grace for Inspiration and Wisdom,
Grace for Understanding,
Grace for Knowledge,
Grace for Loving Kindness,
Grace for Strength and Discernment,

Grace for Truth and Beauty,

Grace for Clear Action,

Grace for Clear Thought,

Grace for a strong, flexible Foundation,

Grace to manifest health and abundance in me, my life and
through me to the world.

Going Down the Central Column of the Tree

Simply draw your hands from Keter down through Da'at to
Tiferet, and then to Yesod and Malkhut.

Words:

From Thee Comes All Grace.

Grace for Connection,

Grace for Gnosis,

Grace for Truth and Beauty,

Grace for a strong, flexible Foundation,

Grace to manifest health and abundance in me, my life and
through me to the world.

Contemplative Prayer

This is a meditative technique used by mystics for millennia and
brought back to consciousness within Christianity in the 20th
century by the American monk and Cistercian priest, Thomas
Keating.

Fr Keating named it "Centring Prayer" and it differs from
regular meditation in that the intention is not just to still the
mind but to open ourselves up to the presence of Divinity. It is
not so much prayer as listening.

Centring Prayer is a powerful release mechanism for both
intellectual side triads because it teaches us the art of letting go
of control and they are all about control. Centring prayer means
to sit in stillness of body, heart and mind with two intentions —
to experience the I AM inside our own I am and to let go of the

images and words that block it. In doing this, we start to collapse the swollen practised belief systems and allow the true presence of God at Keter to reside within us at Tiferet. It means being willing to be changed from above.

When we first start practising centring prayer, just as with meditation, most of us are stunned at how active our minds are and how hard it is to still them. We are also unlikely to hear or experience the beautiful, comforting, strong presence of Divinity for quite some while which can be discouraging. This is about "waiting on God" and that is a discipline which simply has to be learnt. If nothing seems to happen, it is not God refusing to come; rather our souls not opening up as swiftly as we want them to. If we haven't habitually cultivated space and stillness, our soul is automatically shy of new experiences which it fears may be hurtful.

It is similar to putting out food for the birds in your garden and waiting for them to come to eat. Often it seems a ridiculous amount of time before the first bird arrives and then there is an even longer wait before it returns or others come. After all, we know we're not going to hurt them, so why don't they? But birds are shy and wary of predators... and if we believe at any level that God is somehow predatory, it will take our soul a long time to open itself fully to the Grace that is waiting to embrace us.

However, if we continue to commit to taking five... maybe ten... minutes each morning before we start our day in order to practise letting go of our thoughts and returning again and again to our intention of listening for God, a feeling of Grace will first flicker and then delve into our hearts and minds.

Fr Keating recommends that we embrace centring prayer for two sessions of 20 minutes every day but, if you're anything like me, the very thought of that will send you galloping in the opposite direction!

I'd recommend starting off with a maximum of five minutes first thing in the morning, stretching that out over time and then adding a short evening practice, perhaps on finishing work. I began by only doing it on workdays which gave my ego two days off; something that it already understood as a concept. Slowly but steadily, the practice became so engrossing (and even exciting) that my ego agreed to the continuing habit, started to insist that it was done and even to anticipate it as a genuine pleasure.

The Prayer of Grace can also be of assistance when you are sitting in meditation. I like to imagine the ten sefirot of the Tree of Life within my body as I sit. I rise up the Tree and then focus on my crown chakra with the phrase "Grace for Connection". This holds me in higher consciousness and makes it easier to meditate. I continue the prayer back down the Tree when my meditation time is over.

However, if you do plan to try this technique, please start the practice first thing in the morning; maybe even before you get out of bed otherwise it's extremely unlikely that you will get around to it later; the resistance will be too strong, life will roll over your good intentions and there will simply be so many rational reasons why you shouldn't bother...

For me, the process of contemplative prayer brings many challenges. As I let go of thought and relax into myself, I find that flashes of inspiration about the day ahead and new ideas come into my mind and it is tempting to follow or focus on them. Often I want to stop and write them down but that is a temptation that moves me away from the meditative process. It has taken literally years for me to realize that they are simultaneously inspiration and distraction, to allow them, view them and let them go, understanding that if they are true inspiration I will remember them later. Then I return to the intention of sitting in the stillness and waiting. There are many mornings every week when it seems that nothing happens at all apart from my sitting in stillness. Again and again I catch myself off on a train of thought and gently bring myself back up the central column of the sefirot to Keter and the radiant light.

In some forms of meditation, a mantra is useful; a word or short phrase to repeat in our mind which will bring us back to ourselves. This practice, however, like the Prayer of Grace, is to lift us up, again and again, until it becomes a natural process for us to contact the radiance and receive its Glory.

With committed practice, accepting the times when nothing happens as being as important as those when it does, we gradually become able to experience and embrace the Divine within us. There is a knowing, a conviction, that we are with God.

Oddly, that is the critical point when our super ego, super ego ideal and lower ego are quite capable of causing a distraction or creating a valid reason why we have to stop our contemplation practice for sufficient time for us to lose the thread and forget to do it again. Should that happen, please don't beat yourself up; it means that it was truly starting to work! Resistance that powerful is a sign of success. You have got the knack and, if you can restart the process, major beneficial change will now begin.

If we return to—and hold fast to—the practice, all levels of the ego begin to be dismantled and reformed, our side triads lose power and we are able to live more and more from Tiferet, our true self, constantly open to a Divinity that we know, experientially, is love. We begin to be transformed.

The ego, the super ego and the super ego ideal all die when our body dies. That is one of the reasons why we are so afraid of death. If we believe that we are our beliefs, then what is left when we die? The practice of contemplation changes all that. It anchors us into our true self where there is no offence to be taken, no blame to be given, there is simply love.

As a part-time hospice chaplain, I sat with many people who were dying and saw again and again how the process challenged and then, eventually, released the ego's beliefs and thoughts. A slow death is definitely an "ego-ectomy" and, if we believe that we are our ego-selves, then it can be a painful process. If we are centred in our true self, dying is—by the look of it—rather lovely. We see visions of the other worlds and friends and loved ones who have gone before us. Some of us see and speak with angels. We let go of our family requirements and see the people around us with a compassionate clarity. We forgive because we come to know that there is something much greater than what have become petty concerns and our eyes light up with the presence of spirit infusing our souls as our bodies fade away.

We all come closer to our dying every day of our living, so let us do our spiritual practice as if our lives—and our joyful experience of death—depended on it. If we will do the work of allowing the ego-ectomy now, not only can we experience God as the ultimate blessing and strong creative force for good, we will both live and die in joy.

Create a Safe Vessel for the Divine

Many people in spiritual work are in touch with their guides—spirits who advise and guide them—but if you're anything like me, you may find that a bit of a challenge because you're never sure whether you're just making stuff up. Even more concerning is when someone is totally certain of their guide—and the guide was someone important which means that other folk must obey him/her too. All too often that is the ego playing games.

A simple and effective technique to create a vessel to receive divine wisdom is to imagine an animal guide instead of a human one and to let that animal speak to you. If you have had issues around fear of God or condemnatory religion, it might be wise to make it a prey animal, such as a horse or a deer, rather than a predator. A prey animal will be unthreatening at all times whereas our ego could project anger or fierceness on, say, a lion or a panther. However, dog-lovers would most likely be happy with some kind of hound.

This may sound counterintuitive but the idea of having an animal as an imaginary friend who supports you and loves you unconditionally will create an open spiritual vessel for the Divine Dance to be able to communicate with you in a way that you can accept. Imagine the size and colour of the beast. Allow it to tell you its name and discern what its scent might be. Scent is particularly important. Many times I have picked up the scent of hyacinths from nowhere and known at once that my guidance was present and wanted to speak with me.

A wonderful example of this can be seen in Jodi Taylor's novel, *The Nothing Girl* (Accent Press) where Thomas the spirit horse provides company, comfort and guidance to the frightened heroine.

If you would rather experience a human guide, again build a template—see, in your mind's eye, someone real or from favourite fiction that you would *like* to be your guide, whether it's of this era or another so that the Divine can access it. Try not to make it a warrior if you can as healing our relationship with God requires gentleness and softness. However, I, personally, have found the animal concept more reliable.

Whenever you are uncertain, or if you know you are *too* certain, ask for the animal's view and take the first answer it gives; don't second-guess it, that will be your ego interfering. Of course you don't have to take its advice but hindsight may tell you how clear it was.

Many times I've been warned by my beautiful animal that something I wanted to happen wasn't going to, in order to give me time to assimilate and not to react. I still resist that but it's always true and, in retrospect, it helps me see that it was for my benefit.

If you are not visually-minded, use the idea of a very attractive voice through which communication can come.

You'll want to keep this secret, not only because people might mock but because the words "secret" and "sacred" have the same root and the intention here is to have an access point that is unique to, and special to, you alone.

Work out your Hermeneutic

Hermeneutic is a Greek word meaning how you interpret the world and everything in it. It is most often used for those who teach or write about religion so that students can learn what bias or opinions may be behind the teaching.

Our hermeneutics will include beliefs such as Big Pharma is wrong; socialism is right; money is evil; communism is wrong; politicians are corrupt; religion is a way of controlling the masses; my family are good/bad; this diet is the right one; nobody loves me; nothing I do is good enough. They can be bad or good but, if they are unconscious, they will control us and prevent us from seeing anything clearly and dispassionately.

Our hermeneutic about God is particularly important. If it is "God is cruel" or "I hate God" then it is damaging us in some way, not because we are in any way going to be punished for it but because it closes us off from being open to Grace and miracles. That may feel like punishment but it's not from God, it's from us. It is also vital to spot the "God is bad; Source/Spirit is good" hermeneutic because that still means that there is a problem with the religion of your birth or upbringing. If the word "God" still carries such a negative vibration, you will still have some inner block to Grace.

At the heart of all our hermeneutics is one root belief which affects all four relationships. This is sometimes known as The Primal Lie. It will be something like: "I am not good enough," or "What I am is not wanted." It is a LIE and it is usually projected on to our false concept of divinity. It becomes very powerful and it is often this which fuels problems in our emotional side triads creating holes in our auric field that others, mostly unconsciously, will poke. A strong primal lie is a root cause of depression and can even amount to a kind of death wish.

What point is there in identifying it? Anything brought into consciousness starts to lose its power. And it's my experience that the techniques that follow will all begin the process of dissolving your primal lie.

Create an Altar

An altar doesn't have to be a religious thing but it is a very powerful spiritual magnet both for you and Spirit. I like to call them "landing lights for angels." Creating a small corner of one room as a place where you have beautiful and meaningful images on display will help you to remember to connect with the Divine.

On my altar I have:

Fresh flowers.

Four candles (for celebrating Mass).

An olive wood carving of Mary, Joseph and Jesus.

A bronze hare.

Images of Isis and Sekhmet.

Feathers.

My hand-made yod (a tool for teaching).

I add and subtract other items as seem appropriate for the seasons and the services I lead. The wall behind the altar is filled with a hand-painted Tree of Life and Jacob's Ladder, a print of Henry Ossawa Tanner's *The Annunciation*, various icons and a print of Jean Keaton's pencil drawing of Jesus laughing and playing with two Jewish boys.

Creating and maintaining your own altar is a surprisingly joyous experience. Try not to put your coffee mug on it, or dump any filing there. If it is kept for the sacred, it will radiate the sacred.

If you simply don't have a piece of your home that is your own, then create a sacred treasure box. An ordinary shoebox will do, filled with special items that remind you that you are a spiritual being having an earthly experience.

Picture the Divine Mother

Most of our issues with God are with the white, patriarchal God who stares down at us from a cloud. It can be very helpful to put up pictures representing the Divine Feminine, whether it's of Kuan Yin, one of the Marys in the Bible or, perhaps, Isis. When I was sick and realised there was a lot of childhood fear around God still wired into my psyche, I put up a picture of the Virgin Mary with her arms held out and taped a picture of myself, aged six, on to it. The two together looked as though Mary was about to throw her arms around me.

The pictures that we look at are very powerful. Even viewing them unconsciously each day, wires their meaning into our brains. That is why I always suggest reviewing *all* the pictures in your house to see if they represent what you truly want in your life. Images of strife or poverty will never help your brain wire itself into peace and plenty. Images of single people will not draw companionship. When I was younger I had about four big posters of lovely, dramatic-looking women on my walls and I didn't have a single relationship that worked out. Once I took them down, and substituted images of loving couples, my life finally got the hint!

Affirmation

Finding an affirmation to help clear the issues around God can be challenging. Usually I suggest the profound and simple, "I let go and let God" as much to see what kind of a reaction that brings up. If your concept of God is a dangerous one that will bring up fear and discomfort—which will tell you how programmed you are against Divine Love. A good alternative is, "I am open and receptive to all the love and kindness the Universe has for me now."

An affirmation does have to be done frequently in order to carve a new neural pathway in the brain. If we play with this and don't commit, then we won't reap the benefit. Saying an affirmation 100 times when you wake up and another 100 times before you go to sleep is a relatively simple way to start seeing good changes in your life within a couple of weeks. Sometimes, they are almost instantaneous but that's all the more reason to continue as, otherwise, the benefits may fade.

I Am affirmations are particularly powerful because they have the direct contact link with divinity but here is a range that you might like to consider:

- I Am love and I am loved.
- Divine Love is now established and maintained in me and in my world.
- I Am blessed and connected.
- I Am the way, the truth and the life. (This one is incredibly powerful—and yes, this is how we are meant to use it. The Gospel of John's I Am sayings are all intended to help us to draw the Christ consciousness into us, not as emphasis that Christ is separate and conditional.)

I always suggest that the easiest way to do 100 affirmations is to buy a cheap rosary (they are available on the Internet for as little as £3) and run the beads through your fingers twice instead of counting numbers. A rosary has 54 beads so it is easy to say 100 affirmations without actually having to count and risk losing your way.

Some folk instantly react with repulsion at the idea of a rosary because of negative associations with Catholicism. Again, this is a sign of the power of the side triads and the old beliefs within them that are hindering your happiness. Happiness is always in the NOW. You can either let the triads win or take a deep breath and decide consciously to redeem the beads for your own healing.

Alternatively you can, of course, use any bead necklace.

Note: a rosary does include a crucifix. There isn't any problem with cutting that off if you want to. In fact, it might help you to do just that. What a rebellion! Trust me, Jesus won't mind. It may help you to realize that a rosary is not much different from a good-luck charm. Its power is in our belief about it, not in itself. That's exactly the problem we are releasing here: old, set patterns that block our good.

Time Tithing

Any readers of my books on prosperity[3] will know that I am an avid supporter of the mystical interpretation of the Biblical system known as tithing. This has nothing to do with the custom of giving 10% of your income to your church or charity. In fact, the system teaches us to give firstly to God (via people or through things that inspire us), secondly to celebrate life and only thirdly to give to others.

This is the order for tithing according to the Old Testament:

1.   Spiritual Tithe (Leviticus 27:30)
2.   Celebration Tithe (Deuteronomy 12:6, 17–18; 14:22–27)
3.   Charity Tithe (Deuteronomy 14:28; 26:12)

If you want more details on tithing for financial prosperity, please check out my website for a full article on tithing or take a look at one of my books on prosperity.[4]

How tithing works with helping our relationship with God is to ensure that we seek inspiration and then have fun and festivity before we do anything else in life. This is counterintuitive to the three levels of ego which are trained to put everything and everyone else before ourselves.

To time-tithe for healing do the following.

Start each day, and each new segment of each day, by listing ten things in your life that you appreciate. Then give yourself some kind of treat—from a cup of tea to a piece of chocolate or doing something fun. Then—and only then—get on with the business of the day.

Once you have got into the swing of this, increase the number of appreciations to 100 on waking each morning and another 100 before you go to sleep. Please note, these are not gratitudes. Gratitude means that you are thanking someone or something and many of us have programming about that because we all too often have been expected to be grateful for things that we did not want. Appreciation is subtly different in that it is acknowledging joy that you have actually felt.

Again, you can use your rosary to count the 100.

If you are still concerned about finding 100 things to appreciate, here's a starter list for you:

1. My sense of sight
2. The sight of flowers
3. The sight of sunrise/sunset
4. The sight of trees
5. The sight of my partner/child
6. The sight of a smile
7. The sight of my pet
8. The sight of a beautiful landscape
9. The sight of a rainbow
10. The sight of blue sky
11. Books to read (and the ability to read them)
12. My favourite TV show
13. My favourite films
14. My sense of hearing
15. The sound of laughter
16. The sound of music
17. Birdsong
18. A friend's voice
19. The voice of someone I love
20. The sound of waterfalls
21. My sense of smell
22. The scent of flowers/roses/sweet peas/hyacinths/lilies

23. The scent of my lover/child/pet
24. The scent of freshly-mown grass
25. The scent of coffee/bacon/fresh bread
26. The scent of autumn leaves and wood-smoke
27. The scent of the sea
28. The scent of sunshine on my skin
29. The scent of bath oils
30. My sense of taste
31. The taste of a hot cup of tea or coffee
32. The taste of chocolate
33. The taste of champagne
34. The taste of cake
35. The taste of good wine
36. The taste of fruit
37. The taste of vegetables
38. The taste of cool fresh water
39. The taste of potato chips
40. The taste of fresh juice
41. My sense of touch
42. The feel of the heat of a fire
43. The feel of an animal's fur
44. The feel of a lover's/child's skin
45. The feel of velvet
46. The feel of silk
47. Cool fresh sheets on my bed
48. Sunshine on my skin
49. The feel of a hug/a kiss
50. A frosty winter morning
51. A hot bath/shower
52. My body
53. My physical strength
54. My health
55. My skin
56. My flexible hands

57. My breasts/chest
58. My hair
59. My pancreas
60. My stomach
61. My intestines
62. My sexual organs
63. My bones
64. My blood
65. My liver
66. My spleen
67. My legs
68. My feet
69. My heart
70. My lungs
71. My brain
72. My friends
73. My home
74. Happy memories
75. Things that make me chuckle
76. Kindness
77. Birds
78. Horses
79. Dogs
80. Cats
81. Night time
82. Daytime
83. Starlight
84. Much-loved recipes
85. The beauty of falling snow
86. The beauty of frost
87. Rain on parched land
88. The Internet
89. My computer
90. My guardian angel

91. Miracles
92. My telephone
93. My photographs
94. My car
95. Walking
96. Parks
97. Countryside
98. The ability to write
99. My favourite song
100. My favourite clothes

There truly is no excuse for not doing this—only resistance. Even if half of that list appears inappropriate you can think of all the beautiful flowers you can remember, all the good meals that you have eaten, all the good times that you have had, no matter how long ago. A high level of resistance to this is a clear indicator that it is exactly what is needed to start clearing the side triads. You don't want to be programming spirit and yourself with negativity for one more minute of your life.

Clear your *I Am* Clutter

Examine all your negative *I Am* statements and do what you can to cut them out. Most of us have decades of negativity to dissolve by the time a serious dis-ease manifests but this is a powerful tool for change. I Ams are frequently unspoken but implied. "Sorry!" has an implicit I Am as does muttering, "Stupid, stupid." Whenever you spot one, add, "It's okay, I Am safe." It's softly, softly on turning these around. When we are clearing the intellectual side triads it's important not to try and tip the balance dramatically as that will rebound. However, if you want to take this one step further, affirming "I Am safe" 100 times a day with your rosary will be astonishingly helpful as it dissolves much of the unconscious fear we have about any vengeful God.

Spot Your Resistance Principle

Pick one thing you believe passionately is wrong—perhaps an ideological stance, a political party opposed to the one for which you vote, a TV programme you loathe or a religion which you dislike. Find an informed proponent of the opposite point of view on the Internet and listen to them or read their words. Then summarise at least three of their points in writing, adding at the end, "I may disagree, but I acknowledge that I may not know the whole truth of this situation."

Say "I Don't Know"

Very often we don't think about things or situations, we think about what we think about things or situations. Cultivate a habit of saying you don't know whenever you don't have firm personal evidence on a given subject... and even if you do. Letting go of the need to be right is very healing.

Gaze at the Stars

If you have a garden or somewhere safe to do this, wrap up warm on a clear night, go outside and lie on the ground looking up at the stars for at least ten minutes. There is very little better for showing us simultaneously how insignificant we are and yet how integral to everything.

Love Something Without Naming It

When we name something we set our stamp on it and opinions soon follow. One way to do this is to buy a flower or a plant that you don't recognize and resist all attempts to identify it. Or find something in nature that you can't identify and just look at it as it is.

Part Three

Our Relationship with Ourselves

Chapter Eleven

The Soul

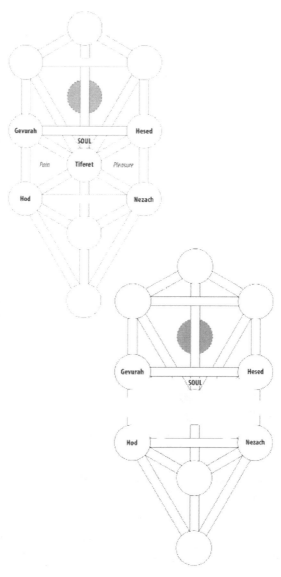

The linking "organ" between all four relationships—with God, ourselves, others and the world—is our soul. Many equate the soul with the heart but it is far more than heart just as mind is far more than brain.

The soul, in Kabbalah, is shown in the triad of Tiferet, Gevurah and Hesed (truth and beauty, discernment and loving kindness). This is the receptacle for spirit and Grace flowing down from Keter through Da'at and transmits both around our psyche and body. I call it the kiss between heaven and Earth.

The three sefirot are the sapwood, the heartwood and the trunk of the physical tree with the sap flowing through Da'at.

This triad is bounded by two emotional side triads of pain and pleasure. Rarely, by adulthood, does a human have a clear and open soul because all four intellectual and emotional side triads are swollen and bleeding through with unhealthy habits and beliefs, squashing the container of the life force we all need for health.

We focused first on our relationship with the Divine, and not with our relationship with ourselves, because the squeezing of the side triads frequently so distorts the soul that we have no idea who we might actually be and therefore cannot perceive who or what to love. Instead, we live from the ego's consciousness—that of who we were trained to be and believe ourselves to be rather than who we truly are. And if we love that, then we are in trouble because it is a distorted mirror.

It is important to become aware of Grace before this stage in order to open ourselves up to Its continual flow. It will then clear enough debris so that we can start to receive miracles, insights and accept that we might have a true self to work on in the first place. Our meditation and contemplative prayer will still the clamouring voices of our programming and allow the healing breath of spirit to cleanse and heal us.

It is important to understand that the human soul is not the area of our psyche which necessarily loves and helps others individually; that is the job of our tribal and family consciousness, lower down the Tree. Our soul is both the individual us and the eternal us. It is greater than the sum of one lifetime and not bound by any persona. There are certainly young souls and old souls and the older the soul, in theory, the wiser it will be. That wisdom will be available to any incarnate human being who is striving to find their true self in this lifetime.

Many people talk of their "soul mate" meaning their lover and friend but a true soul mate is generally the one who challenges us the most, not the one we fall in love with; their job is to help us to grow, not to rest in comfort. The soul focuses on the bigger picture; it knows that our connection with ourselves and with the divine is a reflection of our love for humanity and for the planet. If the soul is not clear, whatever we call love will be ego-centred.

At this level, we may have to say "no" to one person in order to serve a higher purpose for many. Here, we hold the whole Universe in our hand. Our ego, persona and body all fall away when we die but not the soul. The Buddhist *Bardos* teach of how, when we die, we are haunted by "demons" from our unconscious. If our soul is clear and strong, we will see them as being our own negative habits and thoughts personified, let go of them and rise up into the higher worlds. If not, we will run away and swiftly seek a new incarnation to escape what we are experiencing.

This is not Kabbalistic teaching but it is a parallel truth. Hell can only exist in Yezirah, the World of Forms, because hell is all about pain. Kabbalah would teach that hell can only be experienced by a soul which does not know how to rise into the pure light of the heavens. In short, hell is in the emotional side triads.

Before we look at these side triads, let us examine the nature of the Soul itself through the three advisements/commandments associated with its sefirot.

Hesed

Honour the Sabbath and make it holy.

At first sight, this commandment appears to be another about our relationship with God and, in promoting our oneness with the Divine, that is so. But it is more about drawing that divinity into ourselves for our soul's strengthening and it is about our willingness to take care of ourselves for just one day every week so that we can operate at full strength for the rest of the time.

Hesed means both loving kindness and mercy. This is the sefira of the melted heart of forgiveness and acceptance—for all humanity, not just those we love. From here we can love our enemies and do good to those who hate us (luckily we don't have to like them as well!). The only way we can possibly do that is if we learn to love—and transform—the shadow in ourselves first.

When we don't take care of ourselves, we run the danger of running on empty; worse, we may be hypocrites in trying to take the weight off the shoulders of another when we won't take the weight off our own. Misuse of this sefira, ignoring the central column of consciousness, runs unbridled kindness down the pathway to Nezach and into the willingness triad of Nezach, Yesod, Hod. This is ruled by the ego, not the self, and leads to our creating an identity through being "the good one" or "the helpful one" rather than "the inspirational one" who leads others to better pastures.

The mystical interpretation of this commandment isn't about spending a day worshipping in church or temple or even studying the sacred. It is about letting go of the daily round of habits and chores and everything we do on automatic—everything that rules us.

We may already have experienced our soul in meditation or contemplation; when our heart space, our mind space and our body space are all present at the same time in stillness. Then, and only then, we can experience pure presence. It will often be felt as a gentle drop of joy in the heart.

When we learn to take time out in order to be still, we can be content with the present moment and can be intuitive, rational and inclusive all at once.

Contemplation—rather than centring or contemplative prayer—is simply about being in the Now. Even this is not encouraged in our modern world but it is vital in getting to know ourselves. Anything we can't stop doing for one whole day is an addiction and addictions are always contrary to spiritual, mental, emotional and physical health (and they are the driving force of the right-hand emotional triad). In workshops, I always teach the importance of taking a full day a week away from the Internet and mobile phones—and I do know just how hard that can be to do. But once the agitation of the addiction has passed, those are my favourite days. The fact that there still is an agitation and resistance to the idea is exactly the evidence I need that I still have an addiction. I have a wonderful and busy life and it is vital to keep myself fuelled with this downtime so I can be strong for myself and of service to others. Once my Sabbath comes, there is no chance of allowing myself to be at the beck and call of any unnecessary needs of others and I have silence and peace to regroup and re-member myself. And, yes, sometimes other people do find that very annoying!

It is my experience from decades of teaching healing and prosperity work that those who are willing to take a step back one day a week are those who heal and prosper more easily. Apart from teaching us vital self-discipline, a little downtime and silence allows our heart and soul (and God) space to communicate with us and guide us into health.

One lovely lady who told me, "I couldn't not be on Facebook or WhatsApp even for one day a week!" remains sick fourteen years on. That's not the only reason, of course, but her unwillingness to let go of the props she needs to cover up the extent of her problem doesn't help.

Taking space and time out from the everyday world is how we show mercy and loving kindness to ourselves. It's a time for rest, contemplation and thanksgiving but not a time to deny ourselves fun. I'd like to say here that there's no harm in spending that day binge-watching a series on Netflix but that truly depends on the programme you watch. Filling our rest day with images of violence, white dominance, casual sex and enjoying the excitement of vicarious escapism may be huge fun but it is Nezachian fun, not Hesedic, and it certainly does not strengthen the soul.

Anything you read or watch or do that makes you re-member your true self, gives you new insights, lifts you up or simply relaxes you into peacefulness and calm is good for the Sabbath, as is hanging out with supportive and happy friends. It's fine to use adrenaline in horse-riding, climbing, running or the like if you love them because they will refuel you. But this is not a time for hitting the adrenaline button without an active release.

At an even deeper level, the advisement is also about pausing both before and after everything we do; creating conscious space to allow inspiration, understanding and discernment to guide us in what to say or do next. So often, we leap into speech or action before we have considered the content or the outcome of our words and actions. Being consciously present before we speak or act is a service to our own sanity and humanity and an act of love to ourselves and to others.

Gevurah

Honour Your Mother and Father.

"Hang on," I hear you say. "How can this be about my relationship with me? Surely it's about my relationship with my parents."

Externally, yes. Internally and mystically, no. At the soul level, it is all about us.

Family dysfunction flares from generation to generation like a forest fire, taking down everyone in its path until one person has the courage to say, "This stops here and now with me," and extinguishes the flames in their own soul. That person accepts whatever the problem may be within themselves, understanding that we are all one; that no one else has to change; no one else has to sort out the rubbish; no one else is to blame. To bring an issue into the soul brings it to the loving kindness of the sacred masculine and the all-nurturing mother waters of the divine feminine within. Such healing both brings peace to our ancestors and spares the generations to follow.

If we are at peace with ourselves, no one else can knock us off course, hurt us emotionally or cause us to react negatively. No one can push any of our buttons unless we have buttons to push. Therefore the relationship healing needed here is our own.

That is discernment of the highest order. It is only when Gevurah descends from discernment and strength to judgment that it becomes about the others and not about us.

On the surface, the advisement means to acknowledge where your physical parents came from; to understand what emotional loading they were living under themselves as children and how they could only do the best they could with the knowledge they had for their own offspring. It doesn't mean that we have to like them or even stay in touch with them; there are rare occasions when it is a service to both sides to cut off communication, for a while at least.

One of the most powerful books I have ever read is *The Man Woman Book* by Ron Smothermon (Context), which cuts to the quick about the relationship between genders, parents and children. He says the only criterion required of a parent is to raise the child alive. The rest is our desire for them to win a personality contest. Working with that book required huge discipline (another aspect of Gevurah) from me but it opened my eyes to many of my prejudices and beliefs about my physical parents that needed to be healed.

When we sit in judgment (negative Gevurah) on people without accessing Binah, the higher sefira of understanding, we hurt both ourselves and them. Yes, they may have done terrible things but, as the great spiritual teacher, Byron Katie, says, "defence is the first act of war." If we react using the same weapons, the conflict will never end.

It is also worth considering why we chose them for our parents. What is our own responsibility in this? What did we come to Earth this lifetime to learn?

As Kabbalah is comfortable with the idea of reincarnation and karma, it teaches that how and where we come into incarnation is the appropriate place for our particular soul's development and that a soul seeking to develop will make pre-birth agreements with other souls in order to experience what is required for growth. Therefore difficulties with parents, siblings etc. are part of that path and it is our responsibility to honour this. We don't have to like it, we don't have to stick with it but we can and must, at the soul level, use our difficulties to grow and heal and to demonstrate to the world that recovery is possible from even the hardest situation.

When I was having issues with my mother, it was very helpful to hear about her own childhood and realize that she had always thrown me a much softer ball than her own mother had thrown her. However, it was only when I had a life-between-lives hypnotherapy session, which regressed me to a time before my birth, that I realized exactly what the negative and positive karmic links between us were and I could let go, completely, of any perceived problem. In short, it was my karmic duty in this life to be a support system to her, albeit not the dysfunctional one that it was for a while. Even before then, she gave me a marvellous example of what I did not want to grow up to be. It made me fiercely independent but led to many adventures for which I am incredibly grateful.

After my mother had reached the age of 84, a full Uranus cycle—frequently seen by astrologers as a completed lifespan—I became ill with cancer. There were many reasons for that, including being told at the soul level that I had completed my karmic job in ensuring she lived a long and latterly happy life and could either choose to go home myself or rebuild my life by clearing out all remaining emotional debris and starting again with a new impulse.

A friend of mine did not speak to his parents for a decade while he went through intense therapy about his inner demons. He knew that he would project his extreme anger on to them until he had sorted himself out. They did not understand, of course, but his seeming cruelty was a powerful way of rebalancing his own disharmony while honouring them. He was back in touch with them several years before his father died and found that his new insights into himself helped him to navigate the relationship with them astutely, kindly and successfully. And after his father's death, he was able to find renewed understanding as to why his mother had become the woman she was.

As we will see when we look at the pulls of the emotional side triad attached to Gevurah, holding this level of discernment and self-responsibility is rare.

At a deeper level, this advisement is about honouring the masculine and feminine aspects within ourselves and acknowledging the Divine masculine and feminine in all things.

We are all a meld of male and female, whatever our gender, and it is vital that a balance is held so that we have the poise and strength to deal with an unbalanced world run by society's collective Yesod or ego. At the level of the soul, our physical gender is not an issue; it is our ability to maintain equilibrium between giving and receiving, action and reflection, creativity and nurturing.

There is a sacred need to honour the masculine and feminine in the Divine, no matter what orthodox religion may say, and it is entirely likely that religions fall into fundamentalism because the Divine Feminine is lost. The feminine is the inner, esoteric, contemplative, hidden tradition that balances the exoteric, ritualistic active one. The latter is generally all that the Yesodic personality can comprehend. The inner requires deep self-examination and the willingness to embrace and heal our own inner darkness. So, to honour our Spiritual Mother as well as our Spiritual Father is one of the great Holy Grail quests of life. The divine feminine has never been obvious, in-your-face or leading the party; she is the one you have to have the discipline to search for; the hidden jewel, the pearl of great price. And she is hidden in plain sight in every single religious text.

The resurgence of Mary Magdalene in spiritual circles, in mainstream fiction and the popularity of The Gospel of Mary Magdalene is one example of the Divine Feminine bleeding back into consciousness. What is still frequently not seen is how she exemplifies the divine feminine at the time of the crucifixion. She doesn't fight, complain or protest, she and the other women simply go to anoint the dead body of their teacher and are, therefore, the first to know of the resurrection. The angels appear only to the receptive feminine.

Ancient Judaism, at the time of the First Temple, honoured the sacred masculine and feminine and, when it was destroyed and replaced with a more patriarchal faith, the divine feminine still existed in the hearts and minds of the faithful. *"But since we left off burning incense to the queen of the heavens, and pouring out drink-offerings to her, we have wanted everything, and have been consumed by the sword and by the famine"* (Jeremiah 44:18).

The *Fatiha*, the first Sura of the Koran, which is recited by millions of Muslims in their daily devotions, calls Allah *"Al Rahmin"*, the merciful and compassionate one. "Ramin" is derived from the Arabic for "womb" or "matrix", so Muslims are reminded daily that Allah can be either masculine or feminine. What's more, Koranic commentaries describe Mary, mother of Christ, as an intervening force between Allah and humanity. This is characterised by Allah's mercy, forgiveness, sweetness and humility and the embodiment of Allah's love for creation.

When people complain to me about unfairness towards women in religion, I remind them that it is not always the external show of the church or synagogue service that is the heart of faith. In Judaism, it is the woman of the house who lights the Sabbath lights every Friday evening. It may well be that the Sabbath ceremony of wine and bread is held separately later on in winter and that is taken by the man who may then go on to the synagogue for prayers but it is the woman who has drawn down the light of Azilut into the home. She is the bride of the Sabbath, the receptacle of Grace and all the other aspects are far less important than that.

In my own faith, I am an ordained minister in the Independent Catholic church and simply doing the job despite the Roman Catholic church's objections. It seems to me a far better option to find a way to do the work at the grass roots rather than protesting about not being allowed to do the work.

Chapter Twelve

Destroying Ourselves

Tiferet

Do not commit murder.

The Hebrew word usually translated as "kill" is *ratsach*, meaning the wilful act of destruction of a human being. This could indeed refer to destroying another person and Tiferet is the point where our relationship with ourselves melds with our relationships with others. However, anyone who intends deliberately to destroy another has already committed psychological murder against themselves and this is a crucial point.

Tiferet is the Hebrew word for both truth and beauty. Without beauty, nothing is an absolute truth and without truth nothing is authentically beautiful. This can be a tricky concept to take on board in a world where glamour is seen as beauty. Often there is a deep and significant beauty in terrible things—like the love that human beings show to each other in times of crisis. If it is not truthful it cannot be beautiful and if it is not beautiful, it cannot be an Ultimate Truth.

Much of what is presented to us as being beautiful is the human form enhanced by make-up, Botox or even facelifts. While there is nothing intrinsically wrong with any of those, they are not the ultimate truth of the person's physical beauty and frequently hide the evidence of their life's experience which may have given wisdom and understanding. Beauty truly does come from within.

Great truths contain the kind of beauty that inspires awe. A good death is a Tiferet experience, not only for the dying but for those who are present or involved. My father had a heart attack on his way into surgery for a heart bypass operation. When my stepmother telephoned me in tears, telling me, I knew that it was his choice to leave at that moment rather than to go through a procedure that would give him more years of life. Instead of rushing to the hospital, I went and sat in the garden with a bowl of porridge, eating slowly, immersed in the beauty of nature and saying prayers of gratitude for his life. I could see that this was the perfect time for him to leave; my mother, my brother and I were all safe; his work in the world was completed and he was at a peak of personal happiness. When the call came that he had died, I was ready, fed and self-nurtured and able to take on a day that involved negotiating between my mother and stepmother and finding my brother who was away on holiday (in the days before mobile phones or the Internet). Yes, of course, I grieved, and I still do grieve, but there was such simple beauty in that death that I am also at peace with it.

To murder one's self is to allow the side triads to implode upon Tiferet, blocking out both Ultimate Truth and any possible appreciation of the beauty of a situation that the intellect has already judged as wrong. It is self-murder to accept unhappiness as a norm or inescapable. It is self-murder to accept situations that harm us. It is self-murder not to strive to be the best we possibly can. It is self-murder to blame ourselves or others, to self-denigrate, to refuse to give or to ask for forgiveness. It is self-murder to live as the person we were taught that we were rather than the person we truly are. It is self-murder to discount our ideas, dreams or hopes—or those of another. The only one who denigrates the hopes and dreams of another is one who has already immolated his or her self. If you have already cut your own lifeline it will seem natural to you to cut another's—lest they show you up.

It is self-murder to wage war in any way because all war is ultimately against ourselves. To wage war directly against ourselves because we believe we are evil or despicable is the most destructive of actions; it literally tells our blood to boil and our organs to fail.

The Death Wish

Self-murder is the source of the death wish that exists within nearly everyone who experiences a potentially life-threatening illness such as cancer. A death wish takes many years to form but it comprises deeply internalized feelings that life is too hard, that there is no point in trying and that dreams, wishes, personal desires or ambitions have been thwarted or are too difficult to achieve. It may also occur when no desires, dreams or wishes have been considered because the life was subsumed—given totally to others—who have now left home and no longer need the care that is offered.

A death wish takes years to materialize and is nearly always so deeply hidden that the person carrying it would deny it rigorously. It took me many months to locate mine and, when I did, I was horrified at the levels of resentment, jealousy and hatred that were stored deep within my psyche.

Often a diagnosis wakes us up to the rarity, inner truth and beauty of life and we change our attitude and practices, whether we need conventional medicine or not. I can pinpoint the exact moment when I began to recover: I was sitting, wrapped in a rug on the sofa in our living room, in pain and too weak even to walk to the kitchen without becoming breathless. All my ambition, all my plans had gone; I couldn't even cook my own supper. I could barely concentrate on a book or the television. Then I looked out of the window at the birds on the bird feeder which my husband had filled up for me. In that moment, I accepted my life exactly as it was as being more than enough and I was inexplicably, totally content. That was the end of the death wish and the creation of a new life wish.

Within days, healing resources from which I would benefit became available to me and my body began to recover. Once it had true acceptance, it no longer needed to hold all the anger and resentment in pockets of cancerous material so great they were attracting death; it could let go and begin to trust me to be able to reprogramme my patterns into joy.

It's important to emphasise that a death wish does not necessarily have to be a bad thing. It may simply be time to go home and, if that is so, the person will understand this and fade gently away. However, it is frequently the build-up of negative energy to the extent that our soul knows that, if nothing changes, we cannot complete our planned incarnation this time around and is giving us the option to change or go home to try another time. Ideally, the levels of emotional pain we are experiencing will draw our attention to the idea that something is seriously wrong and we may wake up sufficiently to change our lives without a disease manifesting itself. However, the rise in the levels of cancer in the Western world would imply that we are slowly and steadily covering up more and more pain through distraction and denial so that we do not perceive what our soul is trying to tell us until we detect the physical symptoms.

The Triads of Emotion

Just underneath the soul triad on the Tree of Life, either side, are the emotional triads of pain and pleasure. These are the places we run to in order to escape the world when it is too hard. As with all of the triads on the Tree of Life they are neither inherently good nor bad. All depends on the loading we have placed within them. However, because they are fed by our principles and beliefs from the intellectual side triads above and from our thoughts and repeated actions from Hod and Nezach below, they are potentially deep pools of mostly unconscious and destructive passions. The right-hand triad, out of balance, is self-aggrandization and the left-hand triad, out of balance, is self-immolation.

Every "hit" of pleasure or pain that we feel viscerally is lodged in these triads and as they are represented by the watery signs of Pisces and Scorpio too many strikes will muddy and pollute the waters, creating emotional wounds that are both deep and challenging. If you have heard the phrase "a hole in your aura" that would be summed up by damage in these side triads. They are the emotional buttons that others can (and will) push in us. That's why they are part of our relationship with ourselves — it is quite true that other people cannot push our buttons if we don't have buttons to push. No matter what "they" may have done to us, it is our own responses and reactions which are the key and these are generally indicated by our astrological birth chart.

The triads are the places of joy or inner depth, or of codependence, addiction, greed, depression, suicidal tendencies and a deep resistance to letting go and forgiving. Because the triads both touch Tiferet, any wounds and habits within them masquerade as our truth. There may be anger or hatred presenting as our true self or there may be glamour presenting as our beauty self but there may be no real truth nor beauty in either triad.

What is there is a need to feed the addiction, whether it's to pain or to pleasure. Both triads have an energy field of their own — their repeating patterns will show up in life appearing to be external events which have nothing to do with us.

Emotional Triad of Pleasure

Ideally, this is the triad which ensures that we play, have fun and spend time in delight and wonder and, in children, that is exactly how it works. What could possibly be wrong with a triad devoted to pleasure? Unfortunately, for many of us, it becomes our place of avoiding the unpleasant — and the place of being just that little bit wicked. In childhood, this is the place of daydreams and our escape into the fantasy of a book or film. But if life is not happy or our parents are unskilful or addicted in any way themselves, the pattern of running into this fantasy world will become more important and more frequent than it should be. As we grow up if we cannot—or will not—balance the desire for escape and/or pleasure with discipline and ways of dissolving the negativity in our lives rather than running away from it, we will repeatedly head off into whatever sources of relief or pleasure we can find to distract or placate our wounded heart, soul or ego. Once running away becomes a habit, we lose contact with the balancing energy of Gevurah which provides the discernment and discipline to bring us back to truth.

This is the unconscious part of us that drives every single addiction and, if activated, will squash any attempt to stop the fun while turning the fun from a luxury into a vital necessity. If the fun is stopped, then we may start to see the truth at Tiferet and, if the truth is not what we want to see, another hit is required.

This is, of course, seen most clearly in alcohol, drug and nicotine addiction but there are many other ways we can be addicted. Sugar is a common hit, as are social media, exercise, gossip (especially having a good bitch!), sport, gambling, affairs, sex addiction, serial monogamy and binge-watching TV. How do we tell if we have an addiction? Frequently, the truth is that we don't know; once it is lodged in this side triad it becomes pretty much unconscious; in fact we will deny it vociferously if challenged. This is what interventions are for.

If our Tiferet is strong and in touch with Grace, we will be aware of pending addictions and be able to head them off by applying the discipline of Gevurah, both to stop the habit and examine the underlying issue. If not, then we may fall, unaware, into practices and they will begin to rule us. Every writer, musician or artist knows the power of resistance—we will do anything rather than address the discipline of getting down to work—and it is the same with resisting facing up to anything in our lives which needs to be addressed.

The terrible thing about the triad of pleasure is that it takes more and more of the drug of choice to keep us remotely happy so we have to spend more and more time seeking pleasure. And, when we cannot find our fix, then we will be flipped across our psyche's Tree of Life into the very heart of the opposite triad of pain which will feel unbearable. This is the reason why people will steal or even kill to get the hit that they need to escape into pleasure again.

This triad is represented by the astrological sign of Pisces, the positive of which is intuitive creativity and boundless love. Negative Pisces lacks any boundaries and will manipulate subtly to get its own way while appearing to be the epitome of generosity and love. This is not only the negative aspect of addiction, which will cover up its traces from the public eye, but also of codependency which will deny or conceal the addiction of the other.

Emotional Triad of Pain

A balanced left-hand triad of Gevurah, Tiferet and Hod is the aspect of us that carries our conscience, our primal fears, our awareness of how we are treating ourselves and the depths of suffering, whether it's ours or that of another. These are deep emotions, not passing feelings. All well and good—this is a vital check and balance for the triad of pleasure. However, it is all too frequently trained into guilt, fear, hatred, jealousy and self-immolation. This is the root place of diseases such as fibromyalgia which manifest pain and exhaustion without a visible, physical, cause. It is also the location of depression. Bipolar disorder is a seemingly-unstoppable swing between this triad and the triad of pleasure.

The spiritual teacher Eckhart Tolle calls this triad "the Pain Body", describing it as an unconscious entity which needs to feed on more pain drawing more distress to it without our being aware of what is happening.

This triad is the one of what the spiritual teacher Caroline

Myss calls "woundology". The place where our pain becomes our identity. People with a damaged pain triad may say they want to heal but the repeating cycle of hurt becomes so powerful that it feels as if it is part of their survival. To live without it would feel like death because we come to believe that the very illness protects us from having to deal with life. "Oh no, you can't possibly ask me to do that... " This is the pay-off of many diseases and ultimately it becomes a self-perpetuating denial of life.

The pain triad is represented by the astrological sign of Scorpio. Positive Scorpio reaches down into the depths of darkness in order to transform them and heal all wounds. Negative Scorpio is self-destructive, paranoid and secretive, obsessing over the wound as though it were the "precious" of Gollum in *The Lord of the Rings*.

When we are ruled by our deep inner emotions, both these triads will expand or bleed through into our soul, creating a self-perpetuating cycle of wounding and, eventually, may form a death wish. They will almost always cut us off from awakening to a possible greater truth of healing and from our contact with the Divine.

Healing Techniques for Our Relationship with Ourselves

There are thousands of self-healing techniques available for free via the Internet so it will be quite simple to find some that suit you. But here are some suggestions.

Meditation

No, this isn't necessarily the same as Centring Prayer which is lifting ourselves up to meet with the Divine. There are many other ways to meditate and every one of them helps to bring us to our Selves. Meditation is anything which slows our breathing and focuses us on a single point. When we meditate, the natural healing systems of the body are engaged and we feel psychologically at peace. There are active meditations, contemplative meditations and devotional meditations and they can be secular as well as spiritual.

Gardening, dancing, singing, walking, listening to music, watching a butterfly hatch, sunbathing, becoming absorbed in a good book, repeating prayers or affirmations are all good meditations because they pull our minds to one single aspect of life.

Watching TV, being at the computer screen or at the cinema are not meditations because they are external stories being presented to us. Yes, they may be relaxing but they take us out of ourselves instead of settling us within ourselves.

You may be pleased to know that eating a brownie or a bowl of ice cream can be a meditation. You may not be pleased to know that washing up can be one too. In either case, giving 100% attention to what you are doing is the key. To my everlasting surprise, doing our annual accounts has become a meditation for me and there is an unexpected satisfaction in the mathematics of it.

Meditation is about finding yourself; accessing your core-Tiferet. Ideally, we "should" meditate for twenty minutes or so every day but it doesn't have to be the same meditation. All you have to do today is consider the possibilities of what you might consider to be an enjoyable meditation practice and whether it would suit you to ring the changes. Just five minutes a day of complete focus on something is a very good start.

Activate Your Light Grid

The Tree of Life is made up from sefirot, triads and pathways that link the diagram together. This link is to a powerful, free healing technique on the sefirot and pathways from my Kabbalistic colleague, Dr Megan Wagner. Megan is the author of two books on psychology, spirituality and Kabbalah who leads spiritual retreats all over the world. Her work is magnificent.

You may notice in the meditation that Megan and I use different translations for some of the sefirot and you might infer that this means that one of us is right and the other wrong. Not so. One of the most powerful aspects of using Kabbalah is understanding that we all have completely different astrological make-ups and as the pathways of the Tree of Life are always personal (which is why I rarely teach them except in one-to-one situations), different teachers view them slightly differently. Megan is 100% correct in her tradition and I highly recommend all of her work: http://meganwagner.com/products—services/meditations/

Work Out Who You Are

"But I know who I am!" you say. The thing is, we don't. We think we are all the complexes, beliefs and emotions in those side triads.

When I was young, my mother heartily disliked the colour mauve. Every mauve thing which came into sight was disparaged and we soon learnt not to bring anything home which was mauve. From that, I decided that I also did not like mauve. It was a pivotal moment in my life when I finally saw an object which was mauve and realized that I could like it if I wanted to.

Another example would be my uncle who, whenever he was faced with an unknown dish when out for supper, would say to my aunt, "Do I like this, Beryl?" He relied on her opinions so much that he forgot to have any of his own. To be fair to my aunt, this drove her crazy but he was too mired into the beliefs he carried from his parents to be able to come to himself.

We can discover who we are and what we do like through diligent enquiry and by comparing our belief with that of our parents and peers. I like to do it in museums and art galleries. When I realized that I seemed only to like Pre-Raphaelite paintings, I took myself around the museums like the Tate

Modern in London and spent hours just gazing at many images and objects until my true self worked out whether or not I liked them and why. I discovered that I liked to know that an artist understood the concept of perspective, whether or not they used it—and that I could tell the difference. And I found that tiny perception of myself quite fascinating. I also once spent a surprisingly wonderful two hours in one gallery of blue-and-white pottery at the Victoria and Albert Museum, working out what I liked and didn't like about every exhibit. Before I did it, I would have thought that an incredibly boring thing to do but once I had slowed down enough to engage in the meditation of viewing, I was entranced.

Do Something New Every Day

This will both help you discover yourself and encourage your psyche to use and trust Tiferet. As it is only Tiferet that can handle new situations, doing something new every day will strengthen it. This doesn't have to be anything major—simply drinking out of the other side of a cup or putting your right shoe on first instead of your left counts perfectly well. It's a good idea to make this as much fun as possible to engage the ego in supporting you in doing it.

Some suggestions:

- Go into a shop or a museum you have never visited.
- Buy flowers you've not bought before.
- Change a word or phrase you frequently use into a new one. A thesaurus is very useful here.
- Watch a TV show you've never considered watching before.
- Take a new route to work.
- Try food you've not tasted before *and* re-try food you didn't like as a child; your tastes may have changed.
- Put your clothes on in a different order and clean your

teeth in a different order.

- Eat pudding before your main course.
- Dance to a different song every day.
- Decide what you would do with £100,000. If you like, award yourself a new £100,000 every day. Then you can make new decisions as to what you would do with it, having already bought/done stuff with the previous day's money. N.B. Watch out for the temptation to over-give here. It is *not* a game of giving your money away to others every day. Sometimes is fine but if you repeatedly do that, then you are putting out a clear instruction to the Universe that you, yourself, are not willing to receive prosperity.

Practise Ho'oponopono

This is a Hawaiian technique of affirmation using repetition of the words, "I love you, I'm sorry, please forgive me, thank you."

When I first learnt this technique, I was taught that we were speaking to God. I didn't have a problem with that but many people around me did. Instead, I worked out that it is speaking to ourselves—to those pesky side triads and to our ego. The magic of ho'oponopono is that our ego doesn't know who hurt us as it cannot tell the difference between our taking in of a painful thought or belief from one which originates in us. All too frequently an external hurt happens once but we go over and over it until the ego believes that it is a part of our own psyche.

So much of our hurt comes from believing that the other won't apologise and isn't sorry but actually it is our own holding on to the problem that is the issue. I often say that my ex-husband left me once but I made him leave me a thousand times through going over and over the situation in my mind. If we give our power to the others, they—and the external world—will rule us. If we give our power to our True Self, we are the ones with dominion over ourselves.

Ho'oponopono works very simply by understanding that all

unhappiness and pain are caused by the data in our egos, and repeating, "I love you, I'm sorry, please forgive me, thank you," to yourself over and over again until you are virtually saying it in your sleep dissolves this hurtful data and allows good to flow to you. It will help you forgive without even thinking about what you need to forgive and, if you embrace it wholeheartedly, you will find quite swiftly that you can remember something that used to cause great emotion with no attachment at all.

Read and Discover

Falling Upward by Fr Richard Rohr and *You Can Heal Your Life* by Louise L. Hay are the clearest and simplest books I know on our false self (ego) and true self and they will help you discern the difference within yourself. Once we know more about our true self it is easier to find it. Having your astrological chart done or studying the Enneagram will also help as they demonstrate the difference between the characteristics of your Moon (ego) and your Sun (self) and the positive and negative aspects of the number you fit best.

Part Four

Our Relationship with Others

Chapter Thirteen

Awakening

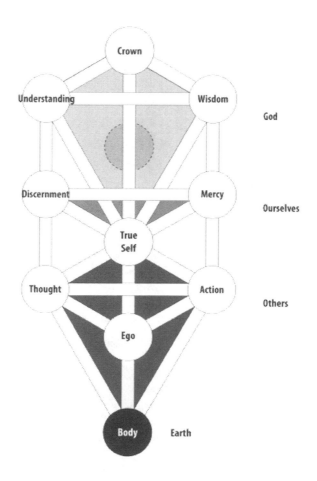

Our relationships with God and ourselves are represented by the top kite of the Tree of Life and our relationships with others and the Earth are represented by the bottom kite. The top kite is united with Spirit in the world of Beriah and the bottom kite is united with physical reality in the world of Assiyah. This is why our relationships with others and physicality seem to be so much more important and powerful; they are manifestly obvious where spirit is subtle.

When we are in balance, both kites are mediated by a strong Tiferet. A good analogy is a rower in a boat, sitting in the centre of the Tree of Life and guiding the craft with deft movements of the oars to move either with or against the flow of the river, according to conscious choice. When we are not in balance, it is as though we are allowing the river to decide where we will end up, whether it is crashing into rocks repeatedly or spinning in circles out of control.

The great secret here is that if we have cleared our relationship with God and our relationship with our self, then there is no need to regard "the other" as anything other than a manifestation of our own creation. Nothing can hurt us or make us sick or afraid without our own participation.

This is, of course, advanced metaphysics but hopefully you will be able to see the possibilities within it.

The lower kite is represented by the astrological sign of Cancer. This is known as the "mother" sign with all the positives and negatives that this implies. Positive Cancer is strong and nurturing, balancing the needs of the self with the needs of others. Negative Cancer is controlling and resentful: "If you really loved me you would..."

Just below Tiferet, and linked to the sefirot of Hod (thought) and Nezach (action), is the triad known as the Awakening Triad. This is the aspect of the psyche which represents individuation— the exploration of who we really are in relation to the external world. It is also known as the triad of ecstasy, the animal triad, the wilderness. Here, we are on the hero's journey or the pilgrim's journey. As the triad is focused on the central column it is capable of balanced consciousness but as it is strongly connected to the physical world it is also heavily influenced by our physical and emotional environments. The tribal consciousness is always ruled by survival so it is impossible for our relationships with the Earth and with money not to be a factor here.

Hod and Nezach are the leaves and the branches of a physical tree. The leaves gather energy (information) and the branches grow according to the value of the nutrition they receive both from above and below.

The Awakening Triad consists of the area between Tiferet, Nezach which represents our active, creative, sensual selves and Hod which represents our thoughts and information. The pathway between Hod and Nezach is known as the liminal line, the point at which we slip between our conscious and subconscious selves. Above it we have, at least, the opportunity to carve our own way in life and below it we are subject to the daily existence and karma of our tribe, our actions and our countries.

The advantage of tribes, countries or herds is that they stick together for safety; the problem with tribes, countries or herds is exactly the same thing.

Ideally, as children we have a family, teachers and peers who are supportive of who we are, create clear boundaries so we can both feel secure and test our individuality against them and can appreciate our unique characteristics. In ancient days in so-called primitive tribes, each child would be observed carefully and given the work most appropriate for him or her to do. This work would become the young person's essential role in the tribe and it would be appreciated, whether it was as shaman or basket weaver.

It is here that we assert our status within the herd, troupe, pack, family or tribe—or decide if we are willing to work with others at all. Some of us are leaders, some are followers, some are healers, some are soldiers, according to our genetic and mental wiring, overlaid by our loading about God and ourselves and others.

When we are growing up and learning about physical life,

this is the triad of our kingship (whichever gender we are). As a healthy child we will play make-believe games of being a prince or a princess, a leader or a warrior as a way of experiencing our own beauty and power. However, we will also allow other children to take their turn as the monarch of all. If we have had a harsh and painful childhood or parents who were unable to teach us self-worth then this triad is weak and unfulfilled or, worse, is fuelled by pain or impulse from the emotional side triads making us either the bully or the bullied.

However, the spiritual seeker is usually a fringe-dweller; someone who lives on the edge of the tribe, seeking new experiences and alternative beliefs. Even in the most secure and stable societies, it is often discouraged when someone wants to strike out on their own especially if their decision is contrary to the rules of the intellectual side triads of that tribe. The primary resistance comes from the belief that "outside" or "the others" are dangerous and that the leaving soul may either be hurt or, worse, may bring destructive forces to damage the structure of the tribe itself.

This Awakening Triad is beautifully described in the Biblical Book of Exodus as being the desert that Moses—the awakening soul—has to enter again and again, firstly alone and then with the tribe of Hebrews who represent the lower part of his psyche around Yesod. The Hebrews are initially interested and excited by the thought of escaping Egypt, which represents slavery in this story, and also by the idea of a covenant with God. But when it comes to committing to the path or keeping to the commandments, they prefer to fall back on the old ways.

So let's divert here and look at that story of the Exodus on the Tree of Life as it will help to explain the whole of the lower kite of the Tree in full before we look at the final Commandments with reference to our healing.

Exodus

The Exodus story occurs after Jacob's and Joseph's descendants, who moved to Egypt in a time of famine, lost their contact with the Divine and sank into a state of emotional and physical slavery. This often happens in religions or faiths when a leader dies and their followers adhere to what was said and taught rather than what is now being transmitted. When we lose our link to spirit, we will hold fast to the law—which will always end up enslaving us.

Moses' part in this begins with Egypt's Pharaoh decreeing that all the male Hebrew slaves should be put to death because they have become too numerous and represent a threat. In a healthy psyche, this would be the body and the mind realizing that there was an imbalance which needs to be addressed. In an unhealthy one, as here, it is the ego and negative Tiferet's pride in wanting to suppress the possible growth of spirituality or the desire for an improved life.

Moses survives because his mother places him in a wicker basket and floats him on the river; his mother has given her son into the hands of the Divine and trusts in Grace.

At the psychological level this is the story of a soul riding on the turbulent waters of emotions rather than just sinking into the karma of the tribe; at the spiritual level, it is a metaphor about how we, individually, can rise above our situation and at the Divine level it is about the destiny of a specific soul.

Pharaoh's daughter rescues Moses, knowing full well that he is a Hebrew child, then pays for him to be raised for his first years in his own loving home and then brings him to the palace to live with her. This is Grace, drawn down through our connection and trust in God.

From then on, Moses receives education as a prince in Egypt which is his first lifting from the ego state into the Awakening Triad. He has to embrace a whole new lifestyle opposed to his first experiences. And while he lives in the palace, he is also aware that he is still part of his birth family and sees that his people are slaves although he, himself, is not. Moses wants to do something about the fate of the others but he is not wise enough yet to be effective. Instead, when he sees a Hebrew slave being beaten by an Egyptian, he reacts. The ego rarely sees clearly and it believes that it can end oppression by attacking the oppressors. Hod, the thought process, makes an automatic snap judgment and Nezach, the active principle, leaps into the fray—here Moses is just as much a slave to his own feelings and drives as the Hebrews are to their physical rulers. Moses kills the Egyptian and Pharaoh plans to kill Moses in revenge meaning that he must leave Egypt to save his life. Heading into the wilderness is the second Awakening. Through his own lack of self-control, impulse and passion, Moses has lost everything and has to start again.

We can see this over and over in our own world where people with good intentions—and bad—react to bad situations and protest or even fight "the other" adding more negative energy to an already bad situation.

Realizing that he is the author of his own downfall, Moses voluntarily crosses the line between Hod and Nezach into the Awakening Triad. He has to realize that in killing the Egyptian to save a Hebrew slave, he was at least as badly behaved as the Egyptian. Yes, he had "right" on his side but two wrongs don't make a right and his actions helped nobody, least of all himself.

Such a crisis means that we are catapulted out of our everyday mindset and have to start thinking in a new way. We have to wake up to new circumstances. This is the opportunity that sickness, bankruptcy or divorce will offer us if we are willing to take it.

Folk in the Book of Exodus spend a lot of time in this wilderness because it is there that we are repeatedly urged to wake up and realize that the ego is never the answer because the ego is always about right and wrong. We can be as right as we like about being sick, oppressed or broke but holding that belief will change nothing. For most of us this takes a good forty years.

The Wilderness

In the wilderness we learn two major things. One, that we have to get over our pride and ask for help and two, that we have to come under discipline. These are the two conscious aspects of Hod and Nezach. An unconscious Hod repeats old thoughts and words, a conscious Hod is willing to learn something new. An unconscious Nezach repeats the same actions—"Another doughnut won't hurt after all!"—a conscious Nezach will change behaviour, "I think I'll eat an apple... my body deserves better nutrition."

The line between Hod and Nezach is "the liminal line". Below it we are subject to all the repetitive thoughts, actions, feelings of the ego but if we learn to live above it, consciously, we become the weavers of our own fate.

Moses, the former prince of Egypt, becomes a shepherd. This is a lesson in humility which is often required on the spiritual path. He goes from being a powerful man, who can command goods, money, obedience and service from others, to a shepherd, who has nothing of his own and has to look after the weakest in order to earn his keep. When we have made peace with ourselves and our problem, then we reach Tiferet, the place of our true self and the aspect of our psyche that Jesus called, "the Kingdom of Heaven". On Jacob's Ladder, this sefira is the crown of the physical world, the centre of the psychological world and the base of the spiritual world. When we are here, revelation can reach us. For Moses it is the voice of the Divine in the Burning Bush. Literally, it tells him to become the saviour of the Hebrew people; allegorically it tells him to save the lower aspects of his own psyche.

Once we have experienced our own Burning Bush of realization we have, like Moses, to go back into the heart of the problem to deal with it properly. In my case, this was to address the root emotional causes behind my dis-ease as lodged in my side triads. As in the case with most of us, the causes were unconscious and not my "fault". Genetics, my parents' mental and emotional states and the consequences of foolish or careless decisions all played their part. But no matter how much the dis-ease was not my fault, if I wanted to change the prognosis I had to become responsible for it and delve deep to find the causes and the answers within myself. The medical profession had been clear that they couldn't cure it; they could only buy me more time. They didn't believe for a moment that it was possible for me to change the prognosis and actively told me it wasn't. Which brings us back to Pharaoh in Egypt.

Kabbalists agree to disagree as to whether Pharaoh represents negative pride (Tiferet) or ego (Yesod). It's probably both. Whichever it is, it is that aspect in us that wants to hold on to the past, the grievances, the habits and discounts anything new, different or unproven. Pharaoh sees himself as the victim for being required to let go of the addictions (addiction is a psychological slavery) that he takes for granted and which give him power.

Pharaoh won't give up one ounce of his control, bringing on himself the ten plagues. To start with he ignores them; they are just passing symptoms; nothing to worry about. And then, when they get worse, he bargains with Moses, saying he will move just a little in the direction asked — and then reneging on the deal the moment the plague is taken away. This is what we often do when allopathic medicine takes away the symptoms of the illness, cuts it out or burns it away. Our brain is designed to return to business as usual and even forget that we were ill and, within weeks, if not days, we are repeating the old patterns which drew the dis-ease to us in the first place.

The Ten Plagues

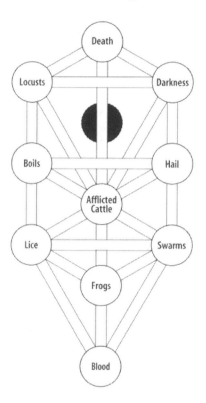

The plagues of Egypt all fit on the Tree of Life, with each one having a slightly more serious and longer-lasting effect than the last. They can be understood in terms of dis-ease as follows:

- Malkhut: The River Nile turned to blood. This represents a digestive disorder. The whole of our living tissue is affected by poisoned water or food but apart from exceptional cases, we can expel the poison and it is generally all sorted within forty-eight hours.
- Yesod: Frogs. These are creatures of water as well as land and represent puffed-up opinions or wallowing in feelings. Physically they would be coughs or colds or swellings. Inconvenient but fairly easy to cover up and ignore.

- Hod: Lice. These represent being eaten by something physical or psychological. Obsessions, skin rashes, itches, fevers. The skin is our largest organ and processes waste. Rashes are a sign of an inner dis-ease trying to come out and cannot be discounted, hidden or recovered from quite so swiftly.
- Nezach: Swarms. This is often translated as "flies" but it could be pretty much anything in excess from discharges to the appearance of mental health issues. Also repeated bouts of illness such as flu or any of the earlier symptoms. The clue is to notice the repetition and how it needs more attention and medicine each time to deal with it.
- Tiferet: Afflicted cattle. Organ damage, diabetes, the first signs of heart disease. Now we are entering the realm of the soul where the warning that we are physically or emotionally off track becomes very clear.
- Gevurah: Boils. A boil represents suppressed anger. This could be the start of a benign or a cancerous tumour. This time the dis-ease is going to hold our attention and there is more chance that we may do something about its cause. Or, like Pharaoh, we may promise ourselves that we will change until the medicine has taken away the symptoms and then forget and continue as before.
- Hesed: Hail. This is the spread of cancer or the explosion of a heart attack. Life-threatening and generally the pivotal chance to turn the tide.
- Binah: Locusts. The stage of illness where no food or medicine can sustain or restore us; we begin to lose weight and approach the point of no return.
- Hokhmah: Darkness. This is the last stage before death; all bodily functions are closing down. At this point, a miracle would appear to be needed; and miracles do happen.
- Keter: Death or transformation.

Return to the Wilderness

You've heard of the layers of the onion theory where we have to go through different levels of the same problem again and again until we reach a final healing. In Moses' case, he may have sorted himself at one level but dragging a whole tribe of Hebrews out of the only life they'd ever known represented a whole new level of problems to resolve. For us, that's when we realize that there is no return to our previous lifestyle. A new level of commitment is required.

In the Exodus story, Pharaoh only agrees to let the slaves go with the death of the firstborn sons of Egypt. But this is only a temporary respite; once the Hebrews have left, he recants again and chases them to the Red Sea—where he and all his army are drowned. That is the end of just one aspect of any disease: it has been destroyed in the present moment by medicine or some dramatic change. But the work of healing mind, body and spirit must continue or the cause of the original dis-ease will ensure that trouble will almost certainly return in a similar or new form—representing in this story by other attacking tribes.

The wilderness is the place where we leave our tribe; it relates to the Awakening Triad on the Tree of Life where we have crossed the liminal line and are living a revised or re-membered life. Often we are without many of the comforts or resources that we used to have—perhaps no alcohol or limited sugar or maybe dealing with the after-effects of illness on our body. We are changing at all levels and this can be very hard for our families and friends to understand. Their resistance alone can be enough to pull us back into the old ways if we fear their lack of understanding. For the Hebrews, this was expressed by repeated complaints that their life in the wilderness was too hard and they would have preferred the "easier suffering" of Egypt where, at least, they knew where their next meal was coming from.

Grace falls for the Hebrews in the form of *manna* from heaven. The Hebrew word manna means "what is it?" and the manna, it is said, fell in the form that was needed for each individual person. For the young and healthy it was bread and meat and for the children and elderly it was softer foods. For us it represents the honeymoon period of our awakening, when we have changed practice, diet or workstyle. But for us, as for the Hebrews, the maintaining of the new practices is hard work.

Over and over again, God makes a covenant with the Hebrews that if they will follow simple rules, they will be looked after. These, to the mystic, are not harsh and seemingly-irrelevant laws but practices of respect for ourselves, each other and the planet. If you read the Bible you will find more than six hundred laws but scholars are clear that many of those are edited in — and the Bible itself states that the Book of Deuteronomy was not "discovered" until about 500 years before Jesus' birth.

It becomes more and more apparent throughout Exodus that the practice of Gevurah is required to achieve spiritual growth and every time the Hebrews renege on their covenant, more restrictions are added. This, for us, is a lesson about listening to our intuition and obeying it — a stitch in time saves nine.

We've already seen that the ten commandments were given to the Israelites three times rather than the generally-believed two. The third time only, they were set in stone.

Each of the covenants and their breaking represents the difference between descending from the soul to the Awakening Triad and rising up from the level of the ego to the Awakening Triad. The former, represented by Moses, shows that our connection with the Divine will bring all the good things that we need to live a happy, comfortable life. The latter, representing the Israelites, means enjoying the excitement of touching Tiferet but then refusing to apply the discipline of Gevurah to maintain our momentum. If, like me, you've ever been a workshop junkie, you may see this in yourself: you go to the workshop and are truly inspired. You go home intending to do the meditation or the affirmations or whatever else was taught but it all falls by the wayside as you get caught up in the everyday cycle of life again. Then you need another workshop to lift you back up into excitement and inspiration.

The Awakening Triad is also the place of science, sport and of politics. This is the area where we strive to excel and will ourselves to become leaders or exceptional people over and above the everyday populace around Yesod. Although conscious cruelty is an almost entirely human attribute, this triad can be ruthless in its bid to achieve its goals just as animals will fight for leadership of a pack or herd. It is the area of scientific achievements because all of science requires proof—and proof can only exist in the physical world. From the Awakening Triad down, we are subject to the physical laws of creation and the consequences of breaking them.

This leads us to the final four commandments.

Chapter Fourteen

The Everyday Commandments

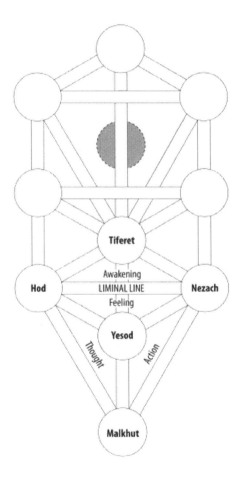

It's a great spiritual truth that you cannot break any of the Ten Commandments without a domino effect that breaks all of the others. This is particularly obvious with the four commandments which circle and embrace Yesod, the ego. Yesod is the bark of our physical tree: what we present to the world.

Yesod is also circled by three triads:

- The Thinking Triad between Hod, Yesod and Malkhut.
- The Feeling Triad between Hod, Nezach and Yesod.
- The Action Triad between Nezach, Malkhut and Yesod.

All three triads are fed by our gut feelings and affected by our physical body. Yesod is the Da'at of the Assiyatic tree, the physical world, so messages are transmitted up and down between the lower psyche and the body.

This is very useful when our body needs to tell us that something is wrong as we will feel out of sorts or disconnected or simply in pain. But psychological gut feelings are reactions rather than responses to life. They point out repeating patterns and if we use them to guide our life we will end up going in circles.

These triads are known as the vegetable level of our psyche, the part of us that runs on automatic. Vegetables grow, have sex, reproduce, seek the sun, age and die; these are all primal urges in human beings, too. However, we are designed ultimately to seek more than this because we are capable of detaching from our automatic settings in order to observe and change.

When we are children we live primarily from these triads, reacting to outside stimuli in order to learn what is safe and what is dangerous. We may touch a hot stove and learn not to touch it again because of the pain but we can also learn to observe when the stove is likely to be hot and when it is safe to touch. We can also learn from being told what to do and what not to do (but like Adam and Eve we still prefer to test it out for ourselves). A cat, on the other hand, if burnt by a stove will never sit on that stove again.

The triads are full of reactionary impulses. These are the things that we do, think and feel without necessarily thinking about them. However, we can stop ourselves reacting from Yesod and its surrounds if we use our conscious mind to consider before we react. I've found that it can take up to six weeks to change a habit at this level but, once it has been consciously done, Yesod will hold to the new as tenaciously as it did to the old. It is Yesod which will make you continue with a practice of meditation, affirmations or going to the gym but you have to be prepared to train it from Tiferet, Gevurah and Hesed first.

Each of us has a preference for one, or more likely two, of these bottom triads and we will customarily react mostly from those. You'll know if you are primarily a thinker, a feeler or an actor. It's thinkers and feelers who programme the pain emotional triad via Hod and feelers and actors who programme the pleasure triad via Nezach. Thinkers and actors are the more practical ones among us who simply get done what needs to be done, perhaps without consulting the feelings of others.

How we can tell the difference between these triads and the upper ones is through our anchoring to the physical world. They are kick-started by our physical senses. A smell will remind us of what we did or how we felt when we first experienced that scent. Something we see or read or hear will also trigger a feeling — or a thought which will lead to a feeling. A certain movement or action will also trigger a thought or a feeling. But all these are transitory. We could feel bad because we haven't had a communication that we wanted and it could trigger thoughts of rejection and make us reach for the chocolate. Then the next time we look at the Internet, the email is there and we feel good, think positive thoughts and, quite possibly, have more chocolate! This is different from the emotional triads further up which work at a far deeper level.

Nezach

Do Not Commit Adultery (Exodus 20:14).

The word Nezach has complicated meanings including Victory and Eternity. This sefira is the principle of action and of excitement. In nature, Nezach is the turning of the seasons: the beginning of spring, summer, autumn or winter—and these are cycles that repeat eternally. They are times when we can feel change in the air and, even though this is a regular occurrence, there's still almost a ripple of excitement in the air. My mother taught me as a child to sense the "turning of the year" in August and I still enjoy watching and waiting for that moment when the robin's song changes and the very scent of the land and its environs is transformed.

So, positively, Nezach kick-starts regular, recurring cycles. Negatively, it is the starting point of the compulsions that lead to addiction. Negative Nezach could be expressed as, "Again, again, more, more, more!" As such, it is the driving force for the emotional triad of pleasure. It is also connected with the lower triads of action and feeling.

When we are coming home from that exciting workshop, we have a choice similar to the game of snakes and ladders. We can stand at Tiferet, reaching out to the strength of Gevurah and we practise positive Nezach by incorporating what we've learnt that is new in our daily routine. Or we let go of Gevurah and slip down the slippery snake to negative Nezach and adulterate what we have learnt.

Webster's Dictionary's definition of "to adulterate" is to corrupt, debase, or make impure by the addition of a foreign or inferior substance or element. For the spiritual seeker, this could mean telling someone unsympathetic all about the work we are doing only to have them denigrate it and pull us out of our joy. Or it could mean having a pizza after an informative session with a nutritionist. We all do things like this because we are human; it's simply important to notice if it becomes a pattern.

We can also adulterate something good in our life by adding more and more to it. Often people will study a healing technique such as Reiki and then add another complementary system to it. This may enhance or it may adulterate it and only conscious thought will be able to discern which of the two it is. The simple question to put to ourselves before automatically going for more is that, if the original practice works, why not just improve ourselves so that it can flow through us ever more clearly? If we look at the stories of the healing power channelled by the first Reiki Masters we can see how strong and clear Reiki can be on its own. However, it is far more tempting and exciting to add more and more symbols or practices which look good on our CV than it is to sit in silence appreciating and consolidating the power of the original. I'm not saying that it's wrong to add other initiations and techniques to Reiki; it is simply important to look at why we might be doing it. If we are disciplined enough to practise self-healing and absent healing every day, together with regular contemplation and/or meditation and we truly feel that we need something else to help, fair enough. But if we are not taking time with the original channelled power then we will almost certainly adulterate it with anything new.

The most commonly understood type of adultery is sexual infidelity and yes, three people in a marriage can certainly be adulterous. However, in rare cases, I have known of marriages where a third element was actually helpful. Again, it is harmful to mix together things that damage each other and only consciousness will tell us whether we are in danger of doing that. It is also fair to say that some marriages of just two people become highly adulterous when they descend into bitterness or lack of communication.

This is basically a commandment about not following impulses without thinking—of remembering to consider and to hold to our true standards. These can be physical, mental, emotional or spiritual. The ego will try to fool us that it is good to look for the new and improved and it just loves to go shopping. The secret here is to observe whether what we want to get actually is new and improved or a rehash of same-old, same-old in brighter packaging.

It is also a commandment about not letting "the other" or their truth impinge on your own reality. Ultimately, if you are clear in your side triads and can view your life from the detachment of Tiferet, you will know that like attracts like so "the other" is simply a reflection of you.

Hod

Do not Steal (Exodus 20:15).

The word Hod in Hebrew means splendour, reverberation and, in Greek, "the way". Hod is the continuation of Nezach — the vibration that maintains the impulse. Things that are splendid are generally of high vibration and Hod maintains them through repeated thought or study. Negative Hod occurs when no new impulse is received or accepted and only the same vibration is repeated. This can lead to paralysis.

Any author will know the importance of having a good editor for their books because an editor will provide Nezach to the author's Hod. Every human being tends to have a limited vocabulary and authors will repeat similar plots written with similar words. An editor, whose range of terminology is different, can make suggestions that lift the text. A bad editor, of course, could be adulterous.

How does this relate to stealing? Hod is entirely rational and logical and yet it is also known as the sefira of the trickster. All mind-games and the magicians' craft are done from Hod and they entertain and reveal magical-seeming things. By making false things seem to be real, they steal truth. "Where's the harm in a little fun?" you may say. None at all, but when the tricks are presented as real or are used to steal dignity, property, information, confidence or reputations, it is another matter.

The media is a Hodian machine, ostensibly a way of spreading information which is of use and a source of vital investigative journalism. However, the media has also stolen careers, lifestyles, relationships and many other aspects of the lives of the people about whom it has written. The healthy nature of Hod is to sift out deception to reveal truth rather than use secrets about the life of another to entertain the masses. Of course, much of this is also Yesodian dishonesty but it can also be information spread that is 100% true but steals all dignity, hope or plans because of the context in which it is given.

It is stealing humanity when we treat another as a thing rather than a person—as in a commodity to sell a newspaper or when only the physical aspect of a disease is regarded as important. In the latter case, it is the disease, not the human, which is medicated. It is also theft when you won't believe that another is capable of doing something and insist on doing it for them instead of teaching them to be self-sufficient.

Physically, to steal from someone else means that you don't believe that you have enough yourself or that you don't have the capability to manifest good for yourself. That way you steal your own dignity and self-respect.

Stealing intellectual property—even nicking images off the Internet—is also negative Hod though our cultural patterns mostly accept the latter nowadays. We can use this sefira against ourselves by stealing too much of our real life with overthinking to the level of paralysis and preferring television, online gaming or use of our mobile phones to actual experiences, preferring to live in a fantasy reality rather than making actual connections.

Negative Hod also takes up too much of other people's time by never stopping talking, instructs when no instruction has been requested, advises instead of listening. It also steals time—and even lives—by insisting that our own negative stories are more important than somebody else's desires.

Yesod

Do not bear false witness (Exodus 20:17).

Yesod is our image, the persona that we present to the world — our mask. Each of us has many masks and each one is partially true but none is totally honest. When we present a mask as being truly us, we are deceiving another and frequently ourselves.

What is fascinating to me is that Yesod is the part of our brain which selects what we actually see, hear and perceive. It does not even present the whole truth to us.

This is a natural defence system which, in ancient days, may have been entirely positive. It still has many helpful aspects because if we did perceive everything around us with our senses at exactly the same level of frequency we would live in a cacophony where we could not focus on anything.

As it is, we zone out what we don't need to see or hear. I'm currently looking at my computer screen and, unless I consciously think about it, am not seeing any of the surroundings. Now that I notice them, there is a window ahead with a garden and fields outside, five plants in the office, an altar with twelve images and candles and a wall behind it with twelve icons and images. And that's not even looking at my desk, the bookcases and cabinets in my office. If I were aware of all of them at the same level all the time, I couldn't focus enough to begin to write.

Yesod learns what to zone into and out of in each of our senses as we grow up. If we are looking for a sign, Yesod will zone in on all the available possibilities which is helpful. But if we have a poverty consciousness, Yesod will zone out opportunities for prosperity. A person with a poverty consciousness literally will not see a banknote in the gutter, for example.

Yesod also runs most of our body's automatic systems. It remembers to breathe while we are asleep and how to get out of bed and walk in the morning. It remembers where we put things (mostly!) and will tell us whether or not we like certain foods.

One of my early exercises when I first discovered the power of Yesod was to retry many foods that I had grown up detesting because I realized that I was still following what might be an out-of-date programming. I discovered that it was perfectly possible to like onions, which I had hated as a child, and also that I could forgive avocados for the fact that I had been eating one when I was twenty and my boyfriend broke up with me. It may or may not be that this pain lodged in my left-hand emotional triad but it was Yesod that remembered that I didn't like the fruit for nearly thirty years because of that one-off association.

This highlights a seeming dichotomy between the three triads around Yesod, which react in the Now, whereas Yesod itself uses information from the past. How this works is that the triads and the sefira of Yesod do all react according to old information but they pull that old information into the present moment and the reactions are generally brief. In all the times that I believed I disliked avocado, it took a moment to refuse it and move on. I didn't remember the moment when unhappiness associated dislike with it or feel the need to dive into that original experience. It was simply a momentarily-activated reaction. Had it been an issue in the intellectual side triads it would have been a case of my believing that avocados themselves were a bad thing and shouldn't be eaten. Some vegans do not eat avocados because farms use migratory bees which is seen as harmful to animals, some vegans say it can't be helped, they are doing their best and eat them anyway and those are intellectual side triad issues.

Neither were avocados themselves lodged in my emotional side triad of pain. When I saw an avocado, I didn't think that it would hurt or harm me if I ate it, it just didn't register as anything I might want to eat.

Perhaps the clearest example of where Yesod can be incredibly out of date is in my craving for custard tarts. (Perhaps I should apologise here for the continual references to food but then I am a Taurean…) When I was very young, and my mother was agoraphobic, I had a carer who would take me to the park in my pram. Mrs Cooper would buy herself a custard tart from the local baker and eat it while she sat on the park bench. She never gave me any and I really wanted some.

Many years later, I ate a custard tart and I don't like them. I still don't like them now (and yes, I do test it out now and then). Nowadays, every time I see one, Yesod still links back to that original craving before reminding me that I don't like them!

Yesod repeats information to us in order to protect us. It needs to be reprogrammed and updated regularly from a conscious Tiferet for us to see the world in a new light. However, doing that is hard work so, generally, we don't bother.

Marketing is an excellent example of bearing false witness. It is a purely Yesodic practice with the goal of making us believe that we have to have that product in order to be better, smarter, stronger, more attractive or more loving. Sometimes that might be true but mostly it is what Kabbalah calls a Lucific truth. The legend tells that Lucifer, Son of Morning, is the fallen angel who envied Adam and preferred to rule in hell than serve in heaven. It is Lucifer's job to test us and he is doing it incredibly well in the modern world through the ruse of glamour. Glamour is a mask made from Nezachian splendour and eternity. It presents people as younger than they are, brighter than they are and clothed in magnificence. It has made us admire women who never age, who are painfully thin and whose faces show not one ounce of character. It has made us admire men who are go-getters, warriors and sex gods. Lucifer can only work through what our Yesods perceive to be beauty, for how could he tempt us with ugliness?

It is also bearing false witness both when we talk things down and when we talk them up. There is a difference, however, between the lie made through pure love and the lie made to impress or to denigrate. Telling a bride at the last moment that she looked fat in her wedding dress—no matter how true it might be—would be the cruellest form of adultery, theft *and* false witness. You would have corrupted her belief about herself, stolen her joy and put your own opinion as being truth. Telling her that she looked radiant would be a far greater truth and a gift of kindness. However, only Tiferet, Gevurah and Hesed can make that decision. Yesod only deals with the old and known even if they are presenting as new and improved. In a time of the genuine new, or in a real crisis, it wires us directly to Tiferet which is one of the greatest blessings there is. If something extraordinary or tragic happens we need to be fully conscious and, in those moments, all our conditioning will be wiped out, even if only for three or four seconds. When Yesod has no data on the matter, or only data which would add to the threat we are facing, it remains silent.

This is why people are able to lift cars off children, out-face barracuda, cope with sudden attack and even death, save someone else's life or move faster than possible with clarity and total lack of fear. They have been kicked into their true selves working to a greater Truth and can—and will—receive Grace.

Healing Techniques for our Relationship with Others

While others may be the obvious causes of harm or abuse we are experiencing, clearing the first two relationships will almost always remove the majority of the external trouble from our lives as if by magic. Once we are filled with Grace and self-love, negativity will begin to give us a wide berth. Of course, we are all works in progress and some outside influences are far harder to avoid than others.

Buddhist Meta Meditation

You will find many forms of this meditation online but its simplest version is to sit in meditation and affirm the following phrases for yourself and then for others.

"May I be safe, may I be well, may I be happy, may I live in peace."

You begin with yourself and then expand the meditation to others in general:

"May all beings be safe, may all beings be well, may all beings be happy, may they live in peace."

Then call to mind someone you love and say,

"May you be safe, may you be well, may you be happy, may you live in peace."

Then turn your mind to people you don't like or who have given you grief and affirm for them,

"May you be safe, may you be well, may you be happy, may you live in peace."

It sounds ridiculously simplistic but sending goodwill to others will change your relationship with them radically and almost overnight.

If you are unwilling to send goodwill to another it is worth considering why that is. Often we feel that we need to hold on to anger or grief because if we don't, we have let the other person win in some way. But to express goodwill is not to condone the behaviour of the other. Like forgiveness, the goal is to set us free from our repeated pain over the situation. The other is far more likely to apologise or make amends if we send them thoughts of goodwill and, if we do it until it becomes a Yesodic habit, we will wear that goodwill in our aura and they will be unable to hurt us again.

Pick up the Projection

Because the ego is all about Me, it projects all our beliefs and practices onto the other. When another offends or hurts us it is because they are highlighting some unacknowledged negativity in ourselves. If you react to another's cruelty or neglect of people, animals or the planet, then it is tempting to be just as cruel to the person you are blaming. I've known perfectly pleasant people call for the death penalty for someone who kept battery chickens and that was an expression of their own inner violence. One of the reasons I have resented women of my age who look perfect is because my ego would like me to look younger and prettier but it won't let me have the work because it believes that it is "wrong". The problem is in me, not in the other, more glamorous women.

So, when you react violently, go within and find the aspect within you which would either like to behave in the same way or *does* behave in the same way. If someone annoys you, find where you do exactly the same thing or wish you could do the same thing. It will be there and, once it comes to consciousness, you will find yourself to be far more tolerant and accepting and, when necessary, you will take appropriate action without over-reaction.

In the modern spiritual world there is much emphasis on the idea of being "an Empath" meaning that you pick up and experience the emotions of others easily. It is worth realising that the original Greek meaning of the word was to project your own feelings on to another and I'd say it's fair to suggest that this is exactly what many Empaths do. Empathy has nothing to do with the soul; it is an expression of the feeling triad between Hod, Nezach and Yesod. Hod is very psychic and the feeling triad is easily rocked, with Yesod loving to add a dose of resentment and self-pity. You may have noticed that physical movement can frequently help when you are perplexed, angry or upset. That is the positive use of Nezach, to balance this triad. Hopefully, Nezach will also encourage action that resolves the original source of the upset.

An Empath is of no use to the healing of others or the world if they are picking up and then perpetuating negative and upset thoughts. So, even if you do feel the emotions of others, intensely, please do ensure that you then work to transform them into healthy and healing thoughts, feelings and, perhaps most importantly, actions. You can't lift the energy of the world through adding more pain to it. Even more, it's important to know that being so sensitive that others can knock you down easily can be a symptom of an unhealthy lack of self-esteem and poor boundaries. Empaths can be very prone to "woundology".

Adopt a Protective Mantra

A good protective mantra which I have often used is, "White light surround me, four angels protect me." Does it work? Yes, because it makes me believe that I am protected and I know that my beliefs rule my life. Do I need it? Almost certainly not but it is a safe and easy habit for Yesod to use if it perceives a memory of a possible threat appearing again. If there is a genuine issue to be faced, I know to move to Tiferet.

You can find many ideas for your own protective mantra online or make one up yourself.

Remove yourself from Harmful Environments

If other people are toxic influences in our life it is only sensible to apply a strong Gevurah and walk away. This is, of course, easier said than done when it is a family member or a work colleague and you can't leave home or don't want to leave your job. However, it is wise not to assume, automatically, that you cannot do either; if you take a clear decision that you will not stay around to be harmed, the Universe will work to support you. It is important, however, to have done self-esteem work, otherwise you run the danger of recreating the same situation with others or even ending up without a place to stay.

However, if there is a critical problem, there are several techniques for protecting yourself from another's harmful influence.

Firstly visualise mirrors facing outwards all around yourself whenever you meet or even think of that person, so that their negative energy is reflected back to them and cannot penetrate your aura.

Secondly, amend your posture to stand up straight with shoulders back and head up and repeat the ho'oponopono mantra in your head. This will change your electromagnetic field and the other will subconsciously change or retreat.

Thirdly, read *The Sacred Magic of the Angels* by Dr David Goddard (Rising Phoenix Foundation), focusing on help from Samael, angel of Mars, the great protective angel. The name, Samael, is often confused with Satan but this is incorrect. Samael is simply the angel of Gevurah who can and will remove you from areas of harm and unhappiness. Samael never hurts the other if you petition for his help; he may even promote the other or bring them blessings; but he will separate you from them.

Many people use Archangel Michael for protection and that is certainly true for matters involving genuine evil. But Kabbalah teaches that everyday protection is not his remit. When it is a mean boss, a thoughtless lover, a bad neighbour or an uncaring former friend, the angel concerned is Samael. Archangel Michael is the Captain of the Host, placed at the Keter of Yezirah, the Tiferet of Beriah and the Malkhut of Azilut and is far too great to deal with such matters. But he won't mind the petition; he will simply pass the request on to Samael who will then protect you without worrying about who gets the credit!

Part Five

Our Relationship with the Earth

Chapter Fifteen

Our Mother, Who Art the Earth

You will have noticed that each section of this book has been shorter than the previous one because if we deal with the biggest problem — our issues with I Am — at the start, then by the process of diffusion, everything else will become easier.

Even if all else fails, physically, clearing that one vital relationship will eventually bring us to a peaceful, even glorious, death where we finally open our eyes to the great glory of Divinity, dissolve our fear of leaving our ego consciousness and our lives and we are filled with the gladness of union. That alone is an incredible healing and one which we would all hope to achieve even if it is not for many years yet.

However, now, we come to our relationship with the Earth. She is our body, the place of manifestation of any and all of the ills that we have experienced in our other three relationships.

As we, as a species, experience the rise of diseases such as cancer, diabetes, asthma and Alzheimer's as well as the non-diseases that appear to demonstrate our ways of adapting to the changes in our environment, such as autism, we can see the same happening with our Mother, the Earth.

The biggest challenges so far to our planet's well-being have come with the advent of science and technology, both of which are locked into Assiyah.

Of course, much of these changes are good but, as we well know, technological and scientific discoveries and advances have also led to oceans filled with plastic, pesticides destroying our vital insect communities, foods that are toxic and fuels that are pollutants.

Where there has been damage, every one of these harmful aspects springs from breaking the last commandment.

Malkhut

Do not covet (Exodus 20:17).

To covet means to envy, to desire what the other has and to want more rather than appreciating what we already have. We covet beauty, wealth, love, land and possessions—and we covet them because we see that somebody else already has them. What we don't realise is that what we manifest (our flowers and fruit on the physical tree) are all dependent on our own inner state and not on any external situation. Certainly the external has influence—and far more than is healthy for us. The external can be represented by the insects and birds that are attracted to our fruits and flowers and whether they pollinate us or pass us by.

Covetousness is greed and it is greed that links each of the ten commandments.

- Covetousness leads to false witness, when we pretend that we have the things that we covet in order to fool ourselves or impress others or we cover up what damage might be caused by achieving our goals.
- Covetousness leads to theft because we will believe that we deserve what the other has and will feel justified in taking our share and we will steal the lives, habitats and foods and supplies of others, human, animal and vegetable, to get them.
- Covetousness leads to adultery because we will experiment wildly to try and get the desired result through cheaper methods, not caring what damage we may cause along the way.
- Covetousness leads to murder both because we will deny that our true selves are enough or that we are capable of manifesting our good from the heavens. It means we will be willing and able take life from another through war or

another form of attack in order to get what we want. Or we may murder them psychologically in order to destroy their achievements and then pick up the pieces for ourselves.

- Covetousness leads to dishonouring our homes and families, our heritage—and the heritage of others—as not being good enough and in dishonouring our planet as a living angelic being in its own right.
- Covetousness leads to overwork, overproduction and over-consumerism as we refuse to allow people, machinery or buildings to rest.
- Covetousness leads to taking the name of the Lord in vain as we will make ourselves and our desires into gods and/ or invoke spiritual power for selfish reasons. Even to try to heal another can be covetousness if we want to take the credit; we call it a "cure" when we have simply hidden symptoms or we are willing to take away the other's necessary life-experience.
- Covetousness leads to graven images such as a face filled with Botox being the cultural norm, war being celebrated as heroic, dictatorships and denial of the fundamental principles of democracy which includes the people's ability to change its mind.
- Covetousness leads to denial of the great I Am by saying, loudly and repeatedly, I Am Not.

When we believe that we are:

- Not good enough.
- Not wise enough.
- Not beautiful enough.
- Not clever enough.
- Not rich enough.
- Not happy enough.
- Not loved enough.

Or any of the other cruel and soul-eating not-enoughs, then we are dis-eased. Looking to the world or its peoples to heal itself or their selves in order to heal our ills for us cannot possibly work.

Our relationship with the Earth is the end result of our relationship with the Source of All, ourselves and others. If, as in shamanistic techniques, we are taught that we are inextricably linked to the Earth then we can see whatever disease she may have as being part of us as well.

Many spiritual beliefs attest to the idea that the Earth is conscious and some call her Gaia. Views differ on whether our planet is an angelic being or a complex mix of living organisms interacting to form a synergy of consciousness. Whichever is true, the Earth is entirely capable of ending the human experiment any time she chooses. At the moment, humanity and its industrial spread appears like a form of psoriasis on her outer crust but the Earth is far greater, deeper and more powerful than her continental plates. She only has to sneeze and thousands of us die. A series of earthquakes worldwide and humanity would be extinct. Then the Earth would take whatever time she needed (and millions of years would be nothing to her) in order to heal.

Kabbalistic teaching is that this may well happen. Humanity as a species is said to be approximately two years old, breaking our toys and having tantrums. It is possible that we will break several planets as we grow up and this may be in the Divine Plan. Should we be expelled from the Earth, we may well begin to incarnate on to another planet which is being prepared for us right now. Of course, that doesn't mean that we shouldn't do all that we possibly can to care for our existing environment and ease the skin disease that we have created.

Religion has some responsibility in this in translating the Hebrew word *radah* in Genesis 1:26 as "dominate" rather than "rule." If humanity dominates the Earth it sees it as inferior. To rule *should* mean to practise *noblesse oblige* — that the leader serves the land through stewardship and respect rather than dictating through greed. The human ego has never been very good at *noblesse oblige*, the soul understands it completely.

Having said that, there is much that we have done as a species to create beauty together with the Earth. Our gardens and our ability to transport different species around the world have created beauty as well as destruction. I often find that when I am gardening, the devas of the land are curious as to what I am doing and, if I explain what and why, they are frequently willing to help. Conscious creativity is exciting for them.

If you are a gardener, a farmer, a tree surgeon or work in any way with the land you can heal your relationship with her by treating her as being conscious. Warn trees or bushes that are to be cut down or back, inform weeds that they are to be cleared, ask plants to let you know what they need to thrive. You might well be amazed…

However, for many of us, a relationship with the land is a rare thing. Our cities and towns pay only lip-service to the Earth and we are frequently cocooned in brick and concrete watching nature only on our screens. When we simply don't know where our food comes from—apart from the shops—then we cannot have a good or healthy relationship with plants, creatures or the land itself. This is the great malaise of our modern times.

One of the reasons that humanity may be experiencing greater mental, emotional and physical health issues may be that there are few places now for newly incarnating souls to learn how to live in harmony with the Earth.

In ancient days, humans lived on, in and with the land and were reliant on the weather and the available food for survival. This generated a deep respect for all creation—and older souls who have incarnated many times will still hold this in their soul. Young souls on their first incarnations may only have lived in urban environments and it is far harder for a soul to grow healthily if its learning processes are all Yeziratic rather than Assiyatic. We may watch *Masterchef* but far fewer of us can cook, let alone preserve or bottle foods. Where once we grew and harvested healing herbs, now we take a synthetic tablet. Yes, there are great benefits from the pharmaceutical industries but they hardly encourage us to take an active part in our healing.

There are many other books which can teach you far more about the environment and its importance to the health of humanity but there are still many ways that we can all re-embrace the Earth, even if we do live in a city. And as the very soil itself is healing to us, it can only do us good to seek the kingdom of Earth as diligently as we may seek the kingdom of God.

Techniques for Healing our Relationship with the Earth

Hopefully I don't even have to mention composting, recycling, cutting back plastic as part of healing your relationship. You may believe that what just one person does cannot amount to much but you are in a one-to-one relationship with the Earth as well as a communal one and to that relationship it makes a *huge* difference what you do each day.

Sing to the Great Mother

My friend, the Dartmoor Shaman, Suzi Crockford, starts each day by singing songs of love and nurturing to the Earth. I sing to the Great Mother when I walk our beagles (though, to be honest, I only do it when other people are not around!). There are many legends that creation was sung into being rather than spoken — for a beautiful account of that, read CS Lewis' *The Magician's Nephew* (HarperCollins). Please ensure you sing positive, encouraging, happy songs; the Earth doesn't need to hear any more of our negativity.

You can make up your own words or tunes or use some of the hymns or songs you might already know. It's quite easy to change the words from "the Lord God" to "the Elohim" if you want to. My favourite is *For the Beauty of the Earth* by Folliott

Sandford Pierpoint.

The first verse (as I sing it) goes:

For the beauty of the earth,
For the glory of the skies,
For the love which from our birth,
Over and around us lies;
Elohim, to thee I raise
This my grateful hymn of praise.

Suggested hymns and songs

1. All Things Bright and Beautiful, Cecil Frances Alexander
2. For the Beauty of the Earth, Folliott Sandford Pierpoint
3. Morning Has Broken, Eleanor Farjeon
4. What a Wonderful World, Bob Thiele and George Weiss
5. Rocky Mountain High, John Denver and Mike Taylor
6. Sunshine On My Shoulders, John Denver, Mike Taylor and Dick Kniss
7. Take Me Home Country Roads, John Denver, Bill Danoff, Taffy Nivert Danoff
8. Ol' Man River, Jerome Kern and Oscar Hammerstein II
9. You Must Believe in Spring, Bill Evans (Michel Legrand and Jacques Demy)
10. Brother Thrush, John Lees

Flower Meditation

Meditating on the ten sefirot of the Tree of Life, visualising flowers or foliage unfurling in each sefira, is a simple and healing meditation which will let you know which areas of your psyche and/or body may need attention and also draw the healing vibration of colour from the Earth to you.

You will find that the flowers you need will come to you but a useful selection would include:

- Malkhut, the base of the spine: A deep red rose or any crimson flower.
- Yesod, the area of your sexual organs: Either bright orange marigolds or soft moon-coloured clematis or lilies of the valley. Orange is the colour of the gonadic chakra but Yesod is represented by the Moon so allow your subconscious to make the choice for you. Vibrant colours lift energy and soft ones soothe.
- Hod, your left hip: Bright yellow flowers such as celandines or buttercups.
- Nezach, your right hip: Scented pink blossom.
- Tiferet, your solar plexus/heart area: Sunflowers to lift energy or a deep pink rose to nurture and heal.
- Gevurah, your left shoulder: Scarlet passion flowers, amaryllis or holly berries.
- Hesed, your right shoulder: Purple scented lilac or anemones.
- Da'at, at your third eye: A cool, soft breeze.
- Binah, your left brain: Salvia, white sage, sea holly or any other plant with soft grey foliage.
- Hokhmah, your right brain: Blue-purple iris.
- Keter, your crown: Pure white flowers such as lilies.

Cording

This is a meditation to draw the healing energy up from the centre of the Earth.

Sit comfortably and visualise a cord reaching down from the base of your spine into the Earth. Experience it growing down through the soil and into the rock, deeper and deeper until it reaches the molten heart of the planet. Now draw this core energy of the planet up through the cord until it flows into your body, filling it with strength and fire.

Feel this energy sink back to the centre of the Earth... then draw up fresh energy. Do this several times until you feel deeply cleansed and strong.

Become a Mountain

Every sefira of the Tree of Life is said to contain another Tree of Life within it. To get into the ten aspects of Malkhut, visualise yourself turning into a mountain. Mountains are like icebergs; we see only their tops but there are great spikes and folds of rock underground so you can feel yourself growing so that your head reaches into the sky while below the waist you sink into the ground beneath you, becoming the bedrock of the Earth. Now experience the slowing down and deep stillness of stone and look deep into your body, observing where you are granite, where you are crystal and where you are sediment and where there are volcanic fires or internal caves and rivers of clear water.

Now feel Grace in the form of rain or snow falling from the sky, covering your top half and easing itself into your crevices to cleanse and heal you throughout until you become a living, moving rock of crystalline light.

Earthing

Earthing yourself is as simple as walking barefoot on a patch of grass. But it does need to be barefoot. When we do that, we return to a symbiotic relationship with the planet which synchronises our consciousness with hers. When we touch the earth with our bare flesh, free electrons from the ground transfer into our body via our skin.

Research from Texas A&M University shows that these free electrons are powerful antioxidants that can help reduce inflammation, help our bodies to heal and improve our heart rate.

You might think, given their contact with nature, that walkers would be the most grounded of people but rubber or plastic-soled shoes prevent us from contacting the Earth's healing energy.

Nowadays we rarely walk barefoot except on a summer holiday at the beach. We don't even lie on the sand—it's plastic loungers on the beach or by the pool.

In 2011, CNN reported a survey in the Netherlands where two groups of people were given a stressful task to complete and then instructed either to sit down indoors and read for half an hour or to garden for the same length of time. The people who gardened reported being in a better mood than the reading group and, when tested, had lower levels of the stress hormone cortisol.

However, if you are unwell or in pain and have the land where you can do it, I recommend full Earthing. That means lying naked on earth—not grass but earth—for up to twenty minutes a day. Obviously you can cover yourself up with a duvet or blanket; it's getting as much of your flesh to touch the ground as you can which is key.

When I was in serious pain with cancer, I found that Earthing on our vegetable patch daily took 100% of the pain away during the times that I was lying on the ground and reduced it for up to six hours afterwards. Obviously that is only my experience but it's worth trying. Except in frost and snow, I still walk barefoot on Dartmoor at least twice a week and it's a joy to feel the ground under my feet.

If you can't get outside, then there are other options. The website www.earthing.com offers cotton bed sheets with silver thread which they claim will give the same effect as lying on the ground. Or you can buy a cotton and silver pad for bare feet under your office desk.

Walk or bathe in Darkness

If you live in a rural and safe area, walk for up to half an hour at night using as little torchlight as possible. On nights around the full moon, you are unlikely to need extra light. Being in the darkness connects you to the heart of the Earth Mother and you will experience deep peace in the silence of your soul. You could sing the hymn, *It Came Upon the Midnight Clear* while you walk.

If you believe in Earth Spirits, you may know that they come out of the plants and trees at night time and they will surely join you on your walk. Talk to them, bless them and thank them. They may feel a little scary—they are not tame and they are, in the best sense, amoral—but hold your ground; you are a human and they do understand that you can be a channel of Grace.

If you can't walk, take a bath in as dark a room as you can for twenty minutes. Let yourself sink into the darkness so that it fills your heart and soul. If you find this frightening it is a sign that you are disconnected from the deep energies of the Earth. Don't frighten yourself but take yourself into darkness slowly or have one lighted candle until you are ready to be in the full depth of the night.

Go to the Country, to a Zoo, a Safari Park or on Safari

I hadn't been to a zoo in more than thirty years until I visited San Diego's environmentally-conscious zoo where species are saved and reintroduced to the wild. It was a revelation to see the animals with my own eyes instead of via a screen. I had quite forgotten the difference.

Seeing or touching a flower, a tree, an animal or a river yourself is to make it real. We are less likely to harm that which we perceive to be real. Of course there are exceptions but if we choose to be angry with those who do kill for fun, we do have to look inside us for where we, ourselves, would like to find an easy target to destroy in order to relieve our own inner hatred and tension. We do not have to condone what they do and it is fair to speak out on the subject but shaming or hating the hunter only shows our own inner imbalance.

Spend Time with a Tree

Tree-hugging is a popular New Age practice but I've always found that sitting with my back against a tree and allowing it to extend its energy field into me in its own good time to be a better idea—I once had a tree tell me quite clearly to clear off when I tried to hug it! This is also a practice that is particularly good to do in the dark. If you can find a strong tree that is at least fifty years older than you are—and preferably one a good hundred years older—and sit in meditation with it through dusk into darkness, then the tree's spirit will come to you. Of course, you may not be able to experience this relationship directly but trust that it is so and allow the strong spiritual sap of the deva to stabilise and ground you. Sometimes you do feel or see the devas—and it is fair to say that they can be quite fierce—so hold your ground and be courteous. Devas, like angels, don't chat but if there is a message for you, you should receive it clearly enough.

If at all possible, sit on the ground rather than on a groundsheet and, if you can, let some of your bare skin touch the tree. Actual physical connection is far more powerful than we have remembered for a very long time.

Go Camping

Simple camping in a tent with a groundsheet isn't for everyone but if you are in a tent by a river, building (safely) your own fire and cooking your own food naturally, it is the most inclusive experience you can have with the Earth. Eating with her, sleeping with her and waking with her are life-changing experiences. If the weather is fine, try to sleep outside, under the stars. We are creatures of fire, air, water and earth and camping brings all four primary elements together both within and without.

Please don't feel overwhelmed by the amount of suggestions. If you just pick *one* and work with it for six weeks, you will have carved an important new neural pathway in your brain which will lead you one important step closer to the healing you are seeking. Every step in the direction of healing is a good step.

May the Grace of Fire, the Grace of Air, the Grace of Water and the Grace of Earth be with you now, and forever, Amen.

Chapter Sixteen

A Life of Miracles

Throughout this book I have woven in stories of my own life experience which I hope have served to show good examples of working with Kabbalah for healing.

Here, I continue the story, in the hope that you will find inspiration, should you come across any similar experiences.

I've always known deep inside that there was something of Grace and Power because of an experience I had had in church at the age of nine.

We were singing the *Magnificat* where the pregnant Mary meets her also pregnant cousin Elizabeth and sings, "My soul will magnify the Lord." As I sang the words, a presence of light, colour, sound, warmth, scent and indescribable beauty embraced me and whispered, "You will do this." The whole experience lasted less than a couple of seconds but it was more real than anything I had ever experienced.

Fortunately, having previously had my head stuck down a lavatory at school for saying that I'd seen a fairy, I was wise enough to keep this vision strictly to myself for more than thirty years. But like Mary, I held it in my heart and I knew there was something magical and mysterious that existed beyond existence.

When my husband, Henry, was dying and that other, exceedingly harsh-seeming, hidden angel of a chaplain said he could not go to heaven because he was not a Christian, he smashed the unconsidered belief system lodged in my religious and philosophical side triads, it reopened the gates of my soul to spirit for the first time in decades and I knew his words could not be true.

I threw my programmed, orthodox Christianity out of the window and, through the process of my grief, began a long journey through other faiths and the New Age to try to find a God that fitted my requirements—a God in *my* image (sigh!). I still believed in the idea of God but Jesus was a complete no-no. How could my husband, who was kinder than I, more generous than I, go to hell when I got to go to heaven simply for signing on the correct dotted line?

I ran away to Australia after Henry's death, lost and confused, with my foundation completely rocked. I wasn't about to commit suicide but I wasn't holding on to life very strongly either and I might not have stepped out of the way of a speeding car.

On my 33rd birthday, I went swimming at the Barrier Reef and, as is often the way when you are unhappy, was repulsed by the delight of the other snorkelers. I swam round the other side of the ship into deep waters... and saw a giant barracuda. Like a fool, I took a photograph of it with my underwater camera. I did not know that barracuda are attracted by light. It turned and started racing toward me with teeth exposed.

I know now that barracuda rarely kill humans but I didn't know that then and I lay in the water, terrified. Just one thought came through, "I want to live." Until that moment, I hadn't been sure.

A Voice cut in to my thoughts very clearly, "Swim forwards and make as much noise as you can. When you get near, hit it on the nose. If it turns, poke its eye with your thumb." And I did the complete opposite of what instinct wanted me to do and obeyed the Voice without thought. I swam straight at the barracuda, yelling under the water.

It flipped away.

I lay there and watched it; it watched me. What did I do next? I wasn't going to turn my back on it. The Voice suggested, "You could swim backwards." I never knew I could do that but I could! When my legs touched the side of the ship I turned and swam round it as fast as I could. Out of the water, I vomited with fear and shook like a leaf.

It didn't click that I was in direct contact with God at that moment and when I got home, I began several years of searching for God through the New Age. Eventually I realized that, although I was happy with Buddhism and general spirituality, there was still a suppurating mass of resentment against Christianity hidden under a figurative pink silk cloth covered with crystals and tea lights in a corner of my subconscious. And what's more, I was broke. There was something deep inside that needed to be healed and I was going to have to go back to the roots and start again.

I enrolled at Birmingham University to study New Testament Greek so I could start reading what the Christian teachings might originally have said and discovered to my horror that there were approximately 32,000 different versions of the New Testament in Greek. It is fair to say that most of them were broadly in agreement but there were certainly enough discrepancies to ensure that this alone wasn't going to take me to the true heart of Christianity.

Then, through the simple miracle of meeting a Jewish man who was as close to the end of his tether over his faith as I was with mine, I was introduced to Kabbalah. Not only did this introduce me to the Judaic mysticism which Jesus would have known but it led me to study the social and economic times of those days. And having some idea of what differing translations there are of the accepted New Testament texts, I slowly began to understand the very heart of Christianity and was able to let go of my anger and my entire belief system so that I could learn to get to know God myself without preconceptions. And I could be at peace with calling it "God" again.

This kind of transformation is the true meaning of the Gospel teaching of being "born again" although a more accurate translation of the Greek would be "born from above". That means you are in direct contact with the Divine, not that you have to take Jesus as your saviour. It's about becoming a mystic, not a Christian.

Once that primal issue was sorted, the rest of my life began to flow better but it wasn't the end of my troubles by far and there was more to unravel before I could even begin to call myself a mystic.

In 1994 I went on a Kabbalistic pilgrimage to Israel. We were a mixed group, visiting Jewish sites which mostly had segregation, and the leader of our group was male. The women believed that the men were getting a fairer deal than they were and by the time we'd reached the Western Wall there was a distinct susurration of resentment going on.

I thought of suggesting that we all got into a circle to pray but didn't follow through because I wasn't Jewish and I was fairly new to the group. Basically, I didn't dare.

That night, in the hotel, the Voice came through to me asking, "Why didn't you speak?"

I answered that I wasn't good enough and I will always remember the reply.

There was a sigh and then the Voice said, "You know what, Maggy? You're absolutely right. You're not 'good enough'. You'll probably never be 'good enough' but you were the only one listening and I can only work with the ones who will listen."

The next day, when the Dome of the Rock was unexpectedly opening late, our group returned to the Western Wall for half an hour and I knew that this time I had to speak up. All I had to do was suggest that we got into a circle and the rest of the women took it from there. And thirty years later on another pilgrimage, one woman spoke movingly on how that synchronistic gathering of the women at the Western Wall had changed her life forever.

My first Kabbalistic book, a novel called *The Book of Deborah* (Tree of Life Publishing), was given to me in one simple Cosmic download later that day at Qumran. I was looking out over where the Dead Sea Scrolls were found and the first chapter and the entire plot just arrived in my head. I raced back to the coach and wrote it down. Later, I tried to change the plot I had been given (it made Judas the good guy). The first time I did that, the file didn't save; the second time, the floppy disk didn't save either. The third time, I got disk boot failure. I got the message. An agent and a publisher turned up right on cue and *Deborah* was published in 1997.

And yet, I still didn't believe I was a mystic.

I'd married for the second time quite swiftly after Henry's death and hadn't had the knowledge to work on the lack of self-esteem which had originally made me choose a terminally-ill man as my first husband. I didn't even know that I was a codependent although my mother had mental health issues and I had spent much of my childhood covering up for and trying (and failing) to be a source of healing for her.

My second marriage ended after an extraordinary adventure where we gave up everything in order to move to Montana, USA, to start a new life. Unfortunately, we didn't give up our deeply-held beliefs that we were not good enough and our venture failed quite dramatically. Still, I became the first person in the world to bring a dog home legally from the USA to the UK on Passport for Pets when it still wasn't, technically, possible. And that too happened because of God. I found myself alone in Montana, in desperate need of a temporary restaurant manager, a veterinarian, a Spanish speaker, a place to stay, a real estate broker, advice on transporting a beagle and a lift to Seattle.

I contacted my Unity minister, Philip Zemke, cried all over him and he told me to get out of God's way. He suggested I stood up at the church on Sunday and asked for everything I wanted. Then it would be time to let go and let God and spend my time relaxing and riding quarter horses in the sunset.

I did what he suggested and, in a group of just 50 people, found a restaurant manager, a veterinarian and a new home immediately. A quarter horse turned up the very next day and everything I needed to get Didcot home unfolded in front of my eyes. I travelled via Spain, where she became a European dog, and six months later I brought her into the UK. I met nothing but miracles of help on the way but my marriage was in desperate trouble. My husband had opposed my bringing Didcot home and our beliefs about the failure of the business and the fate of my dog made the relationship adulterous through our own hardness of heart towards each other.

My intellectual side triads still believed that marriage was for life so I resisted the idea of separation. But one day, in pain and confusion, I gave the relationship back to God in prayer. We had dedicated our marriage to the Divine at the ceremony and I realized that the mystical interpretation of Jesus' teachings on marriage makes it clear that what God has brought together, God may also put asunder. Which God promptly did. My husband met another woman and left me in less than a month and I couldn't even be upset about it! (I was, of course, but I did see the irony in that!)

I learnt much in the years that followed: that my unhelpful beliefs included the concept that I could be wealthy as long as I stayed single but not if I were married; that I was still a codependent which was blocking my self-esteem; and that I had a powerful self-scuppering negative emotional belief about success where I would punish myself emotionally or financially whenever I achieved something valid.

And still there were miracles. I was invited to train for ordination as an independent sacramental priest after doing the funeral of my third (and hopefully last!) husband's best friend, who died saving the life of an elderly woman. At almost the same time, I found that I had developed a mole on my right breast. It stayed dormant until I was approaching the time of ordination—a time which I found very challenging and which brought up quite a few of the old demons about Christianity—

and then grew quickly, became a worrying colour and started to divide. I tried to ignore it (I never said I wasn't a coward!). The night before my ordination, I accidentally scratched it in the bath and it started to bleed.

Very interesting timing. "Okay," I thought, suppressing the panic. "I can't do anything about it tomorrow but I guess I'm off to the doctor pronto."

But as I lay in the bath again, on the evening after the ordination ceremony, having experienced the extraordinary (and known that the Spirit descended into me as my hands were anointed), and contemplating such a wonderful and life-changing day, I noticed something odd.

The mole had gone. Absolutely and completely gone. There was a pale pink patch where it had been and that was all.

It never came back. I don't know if that kind of thing happens often but to me it was a complete miracle with wonderful timing. And I am still very grateful. And yet I still continued to shoot myself in the foot and scupper my dreams.

This was dramatically revealed when I wrote a series of books on Kabbalah. Through not getting oral permissions confirmed in writing and through a primal and truly innocent belief that this work was to be available to the world, I created a situation where I managed to offend the very school that had nurtured me. I was accused of stealing the work of others but this was deeper than that; it was outrage that I, now an ordained Christian minister, no matter how mystical or independent — and a woman to boot — had been published in the mainstream. I was asked to distance myself from the school.

It was a jointly-created situation. Certainly, they walked into my aura but it was my self-scuppering beliefs that manifested the situation in order to prove to myself that I was not permitted to shine. And it turned out to be as great a blessing as that hospital chaplain because, one day when my grief, guilt and anger were so great, I went down on my knees on Dartmoor, in Devon, and begged God to take all my resentment away.

God did just that by wrapping it all up into a blood cancer and manifesting it quite dramatically in my body. Now, this was a very treatable form of cancer and you can live with it for quite some time but my consultant was clear that it couldn't be eradicated and without treatment it would be fatal—and swiftly.

Learning I had cancer was an incredible lesson in humility. My pride took an enormous knock because, without consciously realizing it, I had been judgmental about other spiritual folk who became sick and, up until the book-publishing scenario, I had assumed that because I was well, I was doing everything "right". That was a huge wake-up call for me, especially when I realized that other people did not judge me the way I had been judging them.

As we so often do, I threw myself into the Assiyatic world of healing—juicing, vegan keto diet with long walks twice a day, practices recommended by naturopaths, tests for vitamin deficiencies, a course of enormous doses of vitamin C given under medical supervision—while also undertaking shamanic journeying and healing. I refused chemotherapy because my intellectual side triads believed passionately that it was wrong and my emotional side triads were terrified by the fact that it was chemotherapy, not cancer, that had killed my first husband. This had been confirmed by the registrar at the hospital where he died.

It was a wonderful irony that, when she realized that I was refusing conventional treatment, my consultant offered me a trial on exactly the same chemotherapy as had killed Henry!

What was interesting, in retrospect, was that I had contracted one of the very few cancers which responds very well to chemotherapy—for a while, at least. Even my shamanic practitioner thought I would be wise to have it, even if only to buy me time, but my side triads were adamant.

No matter what I did, the cancer continued to grow (albeit

slowly) because I wasn't learning the lesson that it had brought to me which was that my hatred and resentment of the doctors who had given Henry the fatal doses still ruled my belief system about orthodox medicine and Big Pharma. In short, my pride wouldn't let me believe that doctors could help me.

Eighteen months after diagnosis, despite the fact that the rest of me was amazingly skinny and astonishingly healthy, I contracted shingles which flattened me. Within two weeks, my lungs were flooded so that I could barely breathe and I was in A&E with the stark options—accept chemotherapy, and have a tube inserted into my lungs for daily draining, or die. I surrendered.

Being so very sick honed me in a way I had never previously considered necessary. It brought my focus into the present moment and into appreciation of every breath I was able to take. It also changed me from someone who (pridefully) had said she would never have chemotherapy into someone who would have died without accepting a new point of view and undergoing what I had resisted so fiercely. It all made me realize how utterly unspiritual and unimportant I was; and yet how precious I was to many people whom I had never believed cared for me.

So I let go and let God. Even so, I made it as hard as I possibly could for myself—and on the day of the first chemo itself, I managed to create a situation where the medicine was six hours late in arriving and the friend who had come to hold my hand had to leave to pick up her daughter from school. My husband, Lion, would have dropped everything and come but by the time Karen had to leave, it was too far for him to get there in time, so I was completely alone. That was the ultimate moment of surrender. It was just me, the nurse, the chemotherapy and God.

Halfway through the treatment I got severe pains in my chest and the doctors thought I was having a heart attack... but the Voice said it was just the decades of fear beginning to be dislodged. My heart was fine.

After seven painful months of self-examination, therapy and total surrender of my side triads, I went into partial remission. For me—and only for me—the answer at this stage was not to fight cancer but to listen to what it was trying to teach me: that the part of my body which had formed the cancer was the very one which was designed to protect me.

I had felt unprotected for all of my life and the fear and belief that I was unprotected had led to a cycle of situations where even those who were meant to protect me had attacked me, mentally and emotionally. How could my body not obey that belief?

Careful self-assessment revealed a profound and wonderful truth. Throughout my life, even when people could or would not protect me, God had done so every time. I've only given a few examples in this story but every time, *every* time, I have given up control and asked for help, then the situation has been resolved. Even the manifestation of a cancer that was physically obvious was a protection, to empower me to do the work that I needed to do to heal from the inside out and be able to monitor my progress.

Even with this revelation, I became sick again—almost immediately after I had been offered a scholarship to a conference with Father Richard Rohr at the Center for Action and Contemplation in Albuquerque, New Mexico. Fr Richard had become my primary inspiration in discovering the nature of the Cosmic Christ and I was thrilled to have the opportunity to meet him in the flesh. I had booked the flights, I was incredibly excited and, within days, my lungs began to fill again.

I asked God to show me if I was meant to go. The Voice said, simply, "This is a pilgrimage." And within twenty-four hours I had been offered a stopover in Fort Worth, Texas, where I could teach a Kabbalah workshop which would pay for most of my accommodation costs. I also sold some pieces of jewellery associated with my marriage to Henry and to my second husband with phenomenal ease, which paid for the plane tickets.

So I went. I went with so little breath that I could barely walk more than twenty yards, let alone pull a large suitcase. So I went with a very small suitcase. Manifestly stupid? Maybe, but with total faith.

And every step of the way, I was given help and support and this time I got the lesson. Always, because I had felt so unprotected, I had controlled and organized my life. Now, when I was virtually helpless, I had to let my life help me. I had to let strangers carry my luggage, I had to submit to a wheelchair at the airport, I had to move so slowly that everywhere I went, I saw in detail. Miracle after miracle happened. My Uber driver from the airport insisted on taking me to a supermarket in Albuquerque to get food for the four days I would be there; my motel was next to two perfect eating places; I made a friend on the first day of the conference who helped me throughout. Fr Richard Rohr told me, when I was about to interview him for my radio show, that his dog had just died and my hand automatically reached out to his in sympathy. He kept hold of it. I couldn't have walked all the distance to the interview room if my teacher and I had not been moved to go hand-in-hand.

Surrender, surrender, surrender.

And when I got home, another holistic treatment revealed itself to me—cannabis oil. To take it, I had to break the law which was another intellectual side-triad no-no. Again, I surrendered and a contact appeared out of the blue who could supply it. The oil didn't make me high in a pleasant sense, instead it brought out a load of hidden demons, all of which were ready to be healed. Within six weeks, I was asymptomatic and the cancer has never returned.

I must add here that Non-Hodgkin Lymphoma is not a regular cancer where you are deemed clear after five years; it is one where the doctors estimate that you could survive for about ten years, with chemotherapy, but that's it. So, medically-speaking, I'm still on a waiting game. But I know I am not the Maggy who contracted it and I know in my heart that it has gone.

I still have pain at times—like St Paul's "weakness" this reminds me of who I now am and the journey I am on: it is a constant call back to the Divine. Never again will I be able to forget to connect directly with the Great I Am even if only to say, day after day, "Thank you."

So that is why I have written this book. My experience is that clearing our relationship with God first and being willing to surrender and listen is the greatest healing there is. From that, everything else can and will come, possibly very slowly, but there will be guidance every step of the way.

So, my journey so far is about:

- Clearing the graven images in my right-hand intellectual triad that all Big Pharma and all chemotherapy are wrong. And that Christianity is all wrong.
- Releasing the belief in my left-hand intellectual triad that I Am also wrong; not worthy; not protected.
- Releasing emotional pain from feeling that nothing I do is ever enough and that I must do more and more in order to have a hope of succeeding.
- Releasing the emotional pain of guilt, fear, of being blamed and the pattern of punishing myself through self-immolation.
- Being willing to enter the wilderness and make continual new covenants with God and finally surrendering during the times that I was driven, kicking and screaming, into the wilderness against my will.
- Observing what I think and how it leads to what I feel and how I act and pausing to consider, consciously, whether these are thoughts that I wish to have, feelings that are helpful to me and actions that are beneficial to myself and others.
- Spending time every day appreciating life on this

wonderful planet, spending time with her even if it is only gazing out of the window and doing everything I can to help her and limit my destructiveness towards her.

I'm sure there will be plenty more for me to learn in years to come but now I know that there will be years to come. For me, the great message of the Cosmic Christ, Adam Kadmon, is that God is in this journey with me—and with you. God is not there to spare us the experiences which challenge us and make us grow but to be a part of them with us. We get to live on this beautiful planet together, God and I—and we love, dance, laugh and grieve together. And we enjoy the chocolate together too.

Author Biography

Maggy Whitehouse is an independent sacramental minister, a teacher of Kabbalah in the Toledano Tradition, the author of eighteen books on spirituality, Kabbalah, prosperity consciousness and Bible metaphysics—both factual and fiction—and a professional stand-up comedian. She blends mysticism, humour and inspiration in all her talks and workshops.

Maggy has worked in newspapers, radio, including BBC World Service, and as a television documentaries presenter and producer. She runs a twice-monthly online Kabbalah group..

Maggy is an expert on using Judaeo-Christian mysticism to heal the wounds within religion and on the lives of women in Biblical times including Mary Magdalene and the Old Testament Matriarchs and Heroines.

Maggy has taught workshops across the UK, USA and Europe since 1993. Her comedy career began in 2014 at the age of 56 and she was a finalist in the 2016 Bath Comedy Awards and the 2015 Funny Women Awards.

Both Maggy's mother and her Bishop think she should get a proper job.

From the Author

Thank you for purchasing (and hopefully finishing!) *Kabbalah and Healing*. I sincerely hope you found what you needed in these pages and enjoyed yourself along the way.

If you have a few moments, please be kind enough to add a review of the book on your favourite online site for feedback. Also, if you would like to connect with other books or events I have coming up in the near future, please visit either of my websites or my blog.

https://maggywhitehouse.com

https://treeofsapphires.com

https://maggywhitehouse.blogspot.com

https://www.facebook.com/maggywhitehousespirited

With blessings and many thanks for being a companion on this great spiritual journey,

Maggy

Bibliography

Meditation and the Bible. Aryeh Kaplan, Weiser.

Psychology and Kabbalah. Z'ev ben Shimon Halevi, Kabbalah Society.

The Holy Trinity and the Law of Three. Cynthia Bourgeault, Shambhala.

The Murder of Christ. Wilhelm Reich, Souvenir Press.

Women and Religion in the First Christian Centuries. Deborah F. Sawyer, Routledge.

Patterns of Creation. Stephen Pope, O-Books.

The Hidden Tradition of the Kingdom of God. Margaret Barker, SPCK.

The Mother of the Lord: The Lady in the Temple. Margaret Barker, Bloomsbury.

Entering the Castle. Caroline Myss, Simon & Schuster.

Falling Upward. Richard Rohr, SPCK.

Immortal Diamond. Richard Rohr, SPCK.

The Divine Dance. Richard Rohr with Mike Morrell, SPCK.

Misquoting Jesus. Bart D. Ehrman, Harper San Francisco.

The Man Woman Book. Ron Smothermon, Context Publications.

Intimacy with God. Thomas Keating, Crossroad.

Ibn Arabi's Kernel of the Kernel. Ismail Hakki Bursevi, translated by Bulent Rauf, Beshara Publications.

The Sacred Magic of the Angels. David Goddard, Rising Phoenix Foundation.

Quantum Healing. Deepak Chopra, Bantam.

Suggested Further Reading

The Universal Christ: How a Forgotten Reality Can Change Everything We See, Hope For and Believe. Richard Rohr, SPCK.

The Naked Now. Richard Rohr, SPCK.

Awakening with the Tree of Life: 7 Initiations to heal your body, soul and spirit. Megan Wagner, Veriditas.

The Kabbalah's Twelve Step Spiritual Method to End Your Addiction. Gerald Gillespie, SPI Books.

How to Hear the Voice of God. Susan Shumsky, New Page Books.

Eat, Pray, Love. Elizabeth Gilbert, Penguin.

Temple Themes in Christian Worship. Margaret Barker, Bloomsbury.

Loving What Is. Byron Katie, Ebury.

The Power of Now. Eckhart Tolle, Penguin.

Websites

Adam Simmonds: www.spiritofkabbalah.wordpress.com

Stephen Pope: https://patternsofcreation.com

Jim Larkin and Megan Wagner: www.treeoflifeteachings.com

Michael Hattwick: https://abbatradition.com

Endnotes

1. *See The Mother of the Lord: The Lady in the Temple* (Bloomsbury), and *The Hidden Tradition of the Kingdom of God* by Margaret Barker (SPCK).

2. For more on the *Four Worlds* and the *Four Gospels*, see my book, *The Marriage of Jesus* (O-Books).

3. *From Credit Crunch to Pure Prosperity* (O-Books).

4. *Prosperity Teachings of the Bible Made Easy* (O-Books).

BOOKS

SPIRITUALITY

O is a symbol of the world, of oneness and unity; this eye represents knowledge and insight. We publish titles on general spirituality and living a spiritual life. We aim to inform and help you on your own journey in this life.

If you have enjoyed this book, why not tell other readers by posting a review on your preferred book site?

Recent bestsellers from O-Books are:

Heart of Tantric Sex
Diana Richardson
Revealing Eastern secrets of deep love and intimacy to Western couples.
Paperback: 978-1-90381-637-0 ebook: 978-1-84694-637-0

Crystal Prescriptions
The A-Z guide to over 1,200 symptoms and their healing crystals
Judy Hall
The first in the popular series of eight books, this handy little guide is packed as tight as a pill-bottle with crystal remedies for ailments.
Paperback: 978-1-90504-740-6 ebook: 978-1-84694-629-5

Take Me To Truth
Undoing the Ego
Nouk Sanchez, Tomas Vieira
The best-selling step-by-step book on shedding the Ego, using the
teachings of *A Course In Miracles*.
Paperback: 978-1-84694-050-7 ebook: 978-1-84694-654-7

The 7 Myths about Love...Actually!
The Journey from your HEAD to the HEART of your SOUL
Mike George
Smashes all the myths about LOVE.
Paperback: 978-1-84694-288-4 ebook: 978-1-84694-682-0

The Holy Spirit's Interpretation of the New Testament
A Course in Understanding and Acceptance
Regina Dawn Akers
Following on from the strength of *A Course In Miracles*, NTI
teaches us how to experience the love and oneness of God.
Paperback: 978-1-84694-085-9 ebook: 978-1-78099-083-5

The Message of A Course In Miracles
A translation of the Text in plain language
Elizabeth A. Cronkhite
A translation of *A Course in Miracles* into plain, everyday
language for anyone seeking inner peace. The companion
volume, *Practicing A Course In Miracles*, offers practical lessons
and mentoring.
Paperback: 978-1-84694-319-5 ebook: 978-1-84694-642-4

Thinker's Guide to God
Peter Vardy
An introduction to key issues in the philosophy of religion.
Paperback: 978-1-90381-622-6

Your Simple Path
Find Happiness in every step
Ian Tucker
A guide to helping us reconnect with what is really important in
our lives.
Paperback: 978-1-78279-349-6 ebook: 978-1-78279-348-9

365 Days of Wisdom
Daily Messages To Inspire You Through The Year
Dadi Janki
Daily messages which cool the mind, warm the heart and guide
you along your journey.
Paperback: 978-1-84694-863-3 ebook: 978-1-84694-864-0

Body of Wisdom
Women's Spiritual Power and How it Serves
Hilary Hart
Bringing together the dreams and experiences of women across
the world with today's most visionary spiritual teachers.
Paperback: 978-1-78099-696-7 ebook: 978-1-78099-695-0

Dying to Be Free
From Enforced Secrecy to Near Death to True Transformation
Hannah Robinson
After an unexpected accident and near-death experience, Hannah
Robinson found herself radically transforming her life, while a
remarkable new insight altered her relationship with her father, a
practising Catholic priest.
Paperback: 978-1-78535-254-6 ebook: 978-1-78535-255-3

The Ecology of the Soul
A Manual of Peace, Power and Personal Growth for Real People
in the Real World
Aidan Walker
Balance your own inner Ecology of the Soul to regain your
natural state of peace, power and wellbeing.
Paperback: 978-1-78279-850-7 ebook: 978-1-78279-849-1

Not I, Not other than I
The Life and Teachings of Russel Williams
Steve Taylor, Russel Williams
The miraculous life and inspiring teachings of one of the World's
greatest living Sages.
Paperback: 978-1-78279-729-6 ebook: 978-1-78279-728-9

On the Other Side of Love
A woman's unconventional journey towards wisdom
Muriel Maufroy
When life has lost all meaning, what do you do?
Paperback: 978-1-78535-281-2 ebook: 978-1-78535-282-9

Practicing A Course In Miracles
A translation of the Workbook in plain language, with mentor's
notes
Elizabeth A. Cronkhite
The practical second and third volumes of The Plain-Language
A Course In Miracles.
Paperback: 978-1-84694-403-1 ebook: 978-1-78099-072-9

Quantum Bliss

The Quantum Mechanics of Happiness, Abundance, and Health
George S. Mentz
Quantum Bliss is the breakthrough summary of success and
spirituality secrets that customers have been waiting for.
Paperback: 978-1-78535-203-4 ebook: 978-1-78535-204-1

The Upside Down Mountain

Mags MacKean
A must-read for anyone weary of chasing success and happiness
– one woman's inspirational journey swapping the uphill slog for
the downhill slope.
Paperback: 978-1-78535-171-6 ebook: 978-1-78535-172-3

Your Personal Tuning Fork

The Endocrine System
Deborah Bates
Discover your body's health secret, the endocrine system, and
'twang' your way to sustainable health!
Paperback: 978-1-84694-503-8 ebook: 978-1-78099-697-4

Readers of ebooks can buy or view any of these bestsellers by
clicking on the live link in the title. Most titles are published
in paperback and as an ebook. Paperbacks are available in
traditional bookshops. Both print and ebook formats are
available online.

Find more titles and sign up to our readers' newsletter at
http://www.johnhuntpublishing.com/mind-body-spirit

Follow us on Facebook at https://www.facebook.com/OBooks/
and Twitter at https://twitter.com/obooks